A Short History of

WESTERN PHILOSOPHY

A Short History of WESTERN PHILOSOPHY

Dr Ira Sengupta

Former Head of the Dept and Reader, Dept of Philosophy
Sarojini Naidu College for Women, Dum Dum

New Central Book Agency (P) Ltd

Co-Published by

Bijay Publications

E-mail : bijaypublications@gmail.com

Exclusively Distributed by

Bijay Pustak Bhandar (P) Ltd

90/6A M. G. Road, Bhawani Dutta Lane, Kolkata-700007

✆ : (033) 4605-7856, 8777898576, 8274916104

E-mail : bijaypustakbhandar@gmail.com

NCBA

REGD OFFICE
8/1 Chintamoni Das Lane, Kolkata 700 009, India
email: ncbakolkata@gmail.com

CORPORATE OFFICE
212 Shahpur Jat, New Delhi 110 049
email: delhincba@gmail.com

BIJAY PUBLICATIONS
90/6A M. G. Road, Bhawani Dutta Lane, Kol-7
E-mail : bijaypublications@gmail.com

BIJAY PUSTAK BHANDAR (P) LTD
90/6A M. G. Road, Bhawani Dutta Lane, Kol-7
E-mail : bijaypustakbhandar@gmail.com

A SHORT HISTORY OF WESTERN PHILOSOPHY • Dr Ira Sengupta

First Published: April 2012
Reprinted: July 2016, July 2017, **July 2024**

PUBLISHER • PRINTER • TYPESETTER
New Central Book Agency (P) Ltd
8/1 Chintamoni Das Lane, Kolkata 700 009

CO-PUBLISHED BY
Bijay Publications
90/6A M G Road, Bhawani Dutta Lane, Kolkata 700007

PROOF-CHECKING
Subas Maitra

PROJECT TEAM
Pradip Baidya and Somenath Ganguly

ISBN: 978 81 7381 695 6

Price ₹ 295.00

In memory of
my father
Late Chittaranjan Dasgupta

CONTENTS

PREFACE

istory of Western Philosophy is a vast subject. Had I not been pressed by some teachers nd, specially, by my students, I would not have thought of writing on such a vast subject the fag end of my life. They inspired me to write a book which will be helpful to the reliminary study of history of Western Philosophy.

I have tried my best to present here a short and simple but fair and faithful idea of ome of the Western philosophers. In attempting to cover such a vast subject, it is necessary have very drastic principles of selection. Keeping in mind the young college students f Philosophy Honours and their syllabus, I have dealt here with only the philosophical utlooks of Plato and Aristotle from ancient philosophy, and Descartes, Spinoza, Leibniz, ocke, Berkeley, Hume, and Kant from modern philosophy. There is, so far as I know, no ich book, specially in English. The function of such books as this is not to complete hilosophical education but to begin it. The book is intended to meet the need of such ementary students and general readers and help them to grasp the main thesis and haracteristic outlook of these famous Western philosophers.

The authentic books which I have consulted in writing my book are:

1. History of Western Philosophy—B. Russell
2. History of Modern Philosophy—R. Falkenberg
3. History of Modern Philosophy—W. K. Wright
4. A History of Philosophy—Vols. V and VI—F. Copleston
5. A Critical History of Greek Philosophy—W. T. Stace
6. History of Greek Philosophy—Zeller
7. A History of Philosophy—F. Thilly
8. The Scottish Philosophers—Seth
9. An Enquiry Concerning Human Understanding—D. Hume (Introduction by J. N. Mohanty)
10. Handbook of Kant's Critique of Pure Reason—Dr. R. Das
11. A Critical History of Western Philosophy—O. Conner
12. Locke, Berkeley and Hume—Morris

I am immensely indebted to these books and their writers and have taken help from em as and when necessary. I think my effort will be successful if my students as well as general readers are benefitted from the book.

This book owes its existence to the active inspiration of Mrs. Chhaya Sen, Director of w Central Book Agency (P) Ltd. I owe my gratitude to all the staff members who are hind the publication of this book. As in my previous book on Psychology (which was blished from Central Educational Enterprises (P) Ltd) I have been greatly assisted by husband Mr. S. Sengupta and my grandson Sayan Sengupta.

November 2011
olkata

Ira Sengupta

INTRODUCTION

Philosophy seeks to find out the most fundamental and most general truths of life from a comprehensive point of view. Like science, it appeals to human reason more than to authority. Almost all the questions of philosophers are such—as science cannot answer.

Both science and philosophy demand a rational explanation of life and the world. They differ mainly in their outlook. Science explains truth from one particular point of view, but the standpoint of philosophy is comprehensive. It deals with problems like these "Is the world divided into mind and matter? and, if so, what is mind and what is matter? Has the universe any unity or purpose?" Philosophy dives deep into the problems, and tries to grasp the "whole truth", searches for a single principle with the help of which everything can be explained. But the questions are such that no answer can be found in the laboratory. The studying of these questions is the business of philosophy.

Each subject of human enquiry has a history of its own development. History of philosophy follows the growth and development of philosophical ideas like God, soul, matter, space, time, substance etc. The development and historical connection of the various philosophers is not found in the original writings themselves. History of philosophy takes up philosophical ideas in their historical significance and connections only because the conception of evolution in philosophy is of vital importance to a true conception of philosophy.

In fact, it is difficult to understand the different systems that flourished in different ages as isolated from others. Plato criticised the then prevailing philosophers of Greece. Aristotle criticised Plato. But these criticisms are not the whole truth. Aristotle did not discard Plato, but completed Plato's view, Spinoza's philosophy is incomplete without reference to Descartes. Locke criticised and tried to improve upon Rationalism by introducing a new source of knowledge. Berkeley did not cancel Locke's views altogether, but paved the way to scepticism of Hume. And so it is always.

The speculations of different philosophers are only fragments of the whole truth—which history of philosophy alone helps us to realise.

Plato

(428 B.C.-348 B.C.)

1

CHAPTER

I. Life and Writings

(a) Plato was born in Athens in 428-7 B.C. He came from an aristocratic family. He had an well built body. Like all boys from aristocratic families of Athens he was educated in the best schools of Athens. He was against democracy and used to believe that a state which is not guided by philosophers can never be an Ideal State. This shows his aristocratic and well-educated attitude towards life. During the last eight years of the life of Socrates, Plato was his faithful disciple. In his early youth he was very much shocked with Socrates' trial and death and was disgusted with democracy. He travelled to Megara, Egypt and Cyrene. After a few years he came back to Athens and settled there. This time he stayed in Athens for eight years and wrote many of his books. At the age of 40, he again travelled to south Italy and Cicily and gathered much experience. "In Cicily he attended the court of Dionysius, a tyrant of Syracuse. But here his conduct so angered Dionysius that he put Plato up to auction in the slave market.' Plato narrowly escaped the fate of slavery and came back to Athens. As W. T. Stace puts it: "thus disgusted with both democracy and Aristocracy, he seems to have retired into seclusion" and started on thinking on a perfect state guided by a philosopher-king.

He appeared, now for the first time, as a professional teacher and philosopher and established a school, called Academy, which is known as the 'first university' in the world. For the rest of his life he kept himself busy in philosophical writings and in the management of the school which he founded. His aim was to train and educate a philosopher-king. He died in 348 B.C. at the age of eighty.

(b) Plato expressed his philosophical views in the form of dialogues. His earlier writings are known as Socratic dialogues* e.g., Apology, Protagoras, Creto etc. In Meno, Symposium and Republic he expressed his views on the theory of Ideas, of Ideal State of Justice and of Beauty respectively.

Plato's philosophical outlook was very much influenced by Socrates' view. Socrates aimed at finding out and establishing an objective criterion of knowledge. "The theory of Socretes may be summarised by saying that all knowledge is knowledge through concepts". A concept is a general word that means the common and essential character of a group of individuals of a certain class. It is the class-essence, or the name of a class, e.g., man, horse, cat, tree etc. A concept, being the same thing as definition, is something permanent and fixed. The concept 'man' would still be there even if all men were destroyed and it was real before any man existed. Individuals may vary, but the concept is immutable and identical. This identity in different members of a class is discoverable not by perception but by reason. Reason helps us defining a general idea of 'man'. This is how we get an objective standard of knowledge, according to Socrates. Reason is the only source of knowledge.

II. Plato's Theory of Knowledge

The most significant part of Plato's philosophy is his **theory of knowledge** which lies at the basis of his theory of Ideas. Plato's theory of knowledge is a more refined form of the theory of knowledge of Socrates. Socrates used the method of dialogue in explaining and discovering the ultimate truth of life. Plato accepted this method. His procedure is known as **'dialectic method'**, which is a process of forming ideas (concepts) of the lowest class character, gradually rising to higher and more general and more comprehensive classes, so that, ultimately, a single idea is reached through which all other ideas can be explained, thus discovering a unifying principle behind all ideas to make the world of our experience a comprehensive whole.

Plato opens his discussion on knowledge by telling us first what knowledge and truth are not. He thus refutes the false theories of knowledge that prevailed at his time. The first such false theory is that 'knowledge is perception.'

(a) Knowledge is not Perception

Knowledge is Perception is the theory of Protagoras and the Sophists. Plato claims that perception is not knowledge, nor opinion or belief is knowledge. Even true belief is not knowledge. Plato has discussed these problems in his famous book "Theaetetus".

Plato's arguments against perception as knowledge are:

(1) Knowledge is not perception because according to Plato knowledge must be infallible and must be of something real. If knowledge is perception then it is not about the real nature of a thing; but only its appearance. A stick half-immersed in water looks bent, parallel rail lines appear to meet at a distance. In fact, the straight

* If through conversation, and discussion one can arrive at a correct conclusion on some controvertial topic, then that method may be called Diabetic. It is a method of arriving at truth by reconciling opposite views.

stick does not really become distorted when submerged in water. It only appears to be such—Perception gives us only the appearance of the object. Even the straight stick is appearance, in the sense that the actual stick sometimes looks bent, sometimes straight, according as the medium (air or water) through which it is seen—knowledge gives us the reality behind appearance.

(2) Moreover perception involves contradiction in the sense that the same object of perception appears to have contradictory qualities. We perceive a thing as red now, but as violet under blue light, a thing is heavy to a weak person, but light to a strong person. Which of these contradictory qualities are true? Which are false? If knowledge is perception we have no right to prefer the one for the other.

(3) Consequently the distinction between truth and falsity disappears. So perception is not knowledge. Knowledge, according to Plato, is always true.

(4) Again the object of knowledge is different to different perceivers. Perception depends much on the distance, position, light etc. of the perceiver. A table seems to be rectangular from a particular point of view, and square from another point of view. There is no common world, or common object of all perceivers. Thus knowledge becomes subjective.

(5) In this way if perception is knowledge, truth becomes subjective. What is true for me, may not be true for others. As a result the distinction between truth and falsity is no more.

(6) Plato observes that if knowledge and perception is identical, then teaching, or discussing any problem, argumentation etc. are all in vain. Perception being knowledge, the teacher's knowledge, and the knowledge of the pupil are both true. As Prof. Coplestone observes, what then is Protagoras' justification for setting himself up to teach others and to take a handsome fee for doing it?

(7) "If perception is truth, man is the measure of all things because he is a being who perceives. But since animals also perceive (in their own ways) the lowest brute, must be, equally with man, the measure of all things."

(8) "Again if what appears to me is true, (as is in the case of perception being the same as knowledge) then the doctrine of Protagoras is false, because it appears to me to be false—Protagoras himself must admit that his view is false."

(9) Besides, perception is not pure—Perceptual experience involves **thinking**. When we say that 'This is a cat' I classify the animal with similar animals and discriminate it with other animals like dogs etc. These processes of classification and discrimination are thought-processes. Pure perception is a vague cluster of sensations—not a meaningful whole—knowledge is more than perception.

(b) Knowledge is not Opinion or Belief

That **Knowledge is opinion** is the second false theory that Plato seeks to refute. Belief or opinion, even right, cannot be called knowledge. Wrong opinion is evidently not knowledge. Even right opinion or right belief is not knowledge. It may chance that my belief or opinion turns out to be true. Suppose I believe that it will rain tomorrow. Tomorrow it rains. But still my belief is not knowledge, because I based my belief on intuition or instinc, not on reason—Right opinion or belief may often be a blind guess. According to Plato, it is not knowledge. "To possess knowledge, one must not only know that a thing is so, but why it is so. One must know the reasons." Belief is false when it does not correspond to fact. It is true when it corresponds to facts. But even true belief is not always knowledge, in the proper sense of the terms. May be it is a lucky guess. Belief, when supported by evidence, and rational justification only, rises to the level of knowledge. I may believe that tomorrow it will rain. My belief is not supported by evidence. So even if it comes to be true, and of rains tomorrow my belief is not knowledge. But when the metereological department announces that it will rain tomorrow, it is knowledge, because this statement is supported by sufficient evidences. So even true belief is not knowledge.

Again, opinion or belief may be true or false. But knowledge is always true. Because, the object of opinion or belief is particular things and beings. But the object of knowledge is reality, the Ideas, or the Forms. The false theories being refuted, Plato passes on to the **positive side of his theory of knowledge**. What is knowledge?

(c) What is Knowledge?

It is not perception. It is not opinion or belief. It is not even true belief. What is it? Plato adopts the Socratic view that all knowledge is knowledge through concepts. The concept 'man' does not change with individual human beings. Individual man may come and go, but the concept 'man' remains unchanged—knowledge has for its objects these concepts which are fixed and permanent. These are the same as definitions. Concepts are not subjective. These do not vary with individuals. This gives us objective truth. "Knowledge is founded on reason, and reason is the faculty of concepts."

Plato thus believed that genuine knowledge means knowledge of concepts. But he differs from Socrates when he says that these concepts not only belong to our minds, but they really exist outside our mind. Our concepts are true according as they correspond to the real concepts or Ideas or Forms. Knowledge is for Plato "the correspondence of thought and reality or being."

(d) Four Grades of Knowledge

In 'Republic' Plato speaks of **four grades of knowledge corresponding to four knowing abilities of human mind**. These are:

The first two levels make the level of opinion or belief (perception). The second two levels are supersensible levels of reason.

(1) The lowest grade of knowledge is connected with our imagination. It deals with illusion and dream images of particular things and beings, e.g., the so called knowledge of the image or copy of particular 'man'—this or that man. This level of knowledge is not at all 'knowledge' in the true sense.

(2) The next higher level of knowledge consists in perceptual belief and opinion, e.g., knowledge of a particular man. This we get through perception. Individual man is the copy of the Idea 'man'. Here the object of knowledge is copy of concepts.

According to Plato neither of these two levels are knowledge proper.

(3) The next higher level of knowledge consists in knowledge of numbers and figures as is found in Mathematics and Geometry. Here the knowing ability is understanding or intellect. Which is inferior to reason according to Plato. This knowledge, though rational, is based on some self-evident principles that intellect cannot justify categorically but takes them for granted hypothetically.

(4) The highest level of knowledge is based on Pure Reason. Here we have knowledge of the Ideas or Forms e.g., the knowledge of 'man' in general, or the Idea or Form 'Man'. This knowledge is infallible, and is of Reality.

(e) Allegory of the Cave

In order to explain clearly these fourfold gradations of knowledge Plato uses his famous "Allegory of the Cave", in the Book VII of his "Republic". According to this simple those who have no 'knowledge' in the proper sense of the term "may be compared to prisoners in a cave, who are only able to look in one direction because they are bound and who have a fire behind them and a wall in front. Between them and the wall, there is nothing; all that they see are shadows of themselves and of objects behind them, cast on the wall by the light of the fire. Inevitably they regard these shadows as real, and have no notion of the objects to which they are due. At last some man succeeds in escaping from the cave to the light of the sun; for the first time he sees real things and becomes aware that he had hitherto been deceived by shadows. If he is the sort of philosopher who is fit to become a guardian, he will feel it his duty to those who were formerly his fellow-prisoners, to go down again into the cave, instruct them as to the truth, and show them the way up. But he will have difficulty in persuading them, because, coming out of the sunlight, he will see shadows less clearly than they do, and will seem to them stupider than before his escape."[1] Plato here hints perhaps at the trial of Socrates, Socrates was sentenced to death as he tried to educate the people of Athens and their political leaders.

III. Plato's Theory of Ideas or Dialectic

Plato accepted, without alteration, the Socratic theory of knowledge—knowledge according to him is neither perception, nor belief or opinion. All knowledge is knowledge through concepts. Concepts being fixed as they are identical with definitions, they do not vary from individual to individual as opinion or perception or belief vary. So concepts give us objective knowledge. "Knowledge is founded on reason, and reason is the faculty of concepts."

For Socrates, concepts were mental. These help us in thinking about a whole class of particular things. Concepts, being nothing but definitions, have only a regulative value in thought says Socrates. We compare any animal with the definition of man in order to ascertain whether it is a man. Plato builds upon this teaching of Socrates, a new and wholely un-Socratic metaphysics of his own. He converts Socratic theory of knowledge into a theory of the nature of reality—says Prof. Stace. As B. Russell puts it "There is, however, something of great importance in Plato's doctrine which is not traceable to his predecessors, and that is the theory of ideas or forms."

[1] A History of Philosophy—B. Russell, p. 125

Plato's philosophy was influenced not only by Socrates, but also by the philosophical outlook of Pythagoras, Parmenides and Heraclitus. As B. Russell puts it—from Pythagoras Plato derived the religious trend, the belief in immortality, the other- worldliness, his respect for mathematics and also that is involved in the simile of the cave. From Parminides he derived the belief that reality is eternal and that all change must be illusory. From Heraclitus he derived the negative doctrine that there is nothing permanent in the sensible world. From a combination of all these, Plato built up his own system of philosophy in which the most important part is that sense-experience does not give us knowledge. Knowledge is only to be achieved by intellect. As we have seen before, his theory of knowledge, lies at the basis of his Theory of Ideas.

"The later part of Book V to the end of Book VII of Plato's Republic is occupied mainly with questions of pure philosophy. This part is most influential and most famous part of the Republic." **Plato's Theory of Ideas or Forms is partly logical and partly metaphysical.** The logical part deals with the meaning of general words. There are many animals of which some are called "cats". What do we mean by 'cat'? The word 'cat' means something which is different from each particular cat. An animal is a cat because it has the common and essential character of catness. Language needs these general words (like cat) to mean different classes of things, not this or that particular thing. An Idea means this class-essence. This general word is not born when a particular cat is born, and does not die when it dies. In fact, it is not in space and time, it is eternal. This logical part of the doctrine is independent of the metaphysical part, which deals with the theory that the word 'cat' means a certain ideal cat, "the cat" created by God and unique-particular cats are copies of 'the cat', but more or less imperfect copies. It is only due to this imperfection that particulars are many. The cat is real, the particular cats are appearances. In this last book of the Republic Plato explains his theory of Ideas very clearly.

Here Plato explains that wherever a number of individuals have a common name they have also a common 'idea' or 'form'. For instance, though there are many tables there is only one "idea" or 'form' of a table. Just as a reflection of a table in mirror is only apparent and not 'real', the various particular 'tables' are unreal, being only copies of the 'idea' Table which is the only real table and is made by God. Of this one table, made by God, there can be knowledge, but in respect of many tables made by carpenters, there can be only opinion. A philosopher wants to know the truth, the ultimate reality or in Plato's language the Idea or Form or the Universal. The common man wants to know the appearance only.

Plato's Theory of Ideas is unique in the sense that his theory is the theory of the objectivity of concepts. That the concept e.g., "man", is not merely an idea in the mind but something which has a reality of its own, outside and independent of the mind—This is the essence of the philosophy of Plato. Plato, thus, is both an Idealist and a Realist. Plato is an Idealist in the sense that only Ideas are real and nothing else. Ideas only exist. But Plato is a realist also, in the sense that, Ideas do not depend for

*History of Philosophy—B. Russell, p. 121

this existence on human mind, but they are self-existent. Plato's Theory of Ideas is the theory of the objectivity of concepts.

Truth is Correspondence

This theory is based on the view that truth means the **correspondence of our ideas with facts of existence or reality.** If I see a mountain, and if there really is such a mountain, then my idea is true. But if there is no mountain, my idea is false. It is dream, or illusion or hallucination—a product of imagination, not knowledge. Falsehood consists in having an idea which is not a copy of anything existing (real). Now, knowledge is knowledge of concepts. A concept is true knowledge only when it corresponds to an objective reality. So, there must be general ideas or concepts outside my mind. Plato gives the technical name "Ideas" to these real entities, to which our concepts correspond. This and that particular beautiful thing have no reality. Reality belongs only to the idea of Beauty in general.

Plato explains this point thus: there are many beautiful things. The fresh red flower is beautiful, a young woman's face is beautiful, the moonlight is beautiful. All are different. Yet they are similar to each other. Our senses cannot give us this similarity, because it involves comparison and comparison is an act of the mind, not of the senses. So the idea of beauty is in our mind with which we compare beautiful thing and recognise them as resembling our a priori idea of beauty in our mind. Now, either this idea corresponds to something outside us, or do not. In the latter case, our idea of beauty is a figment of imagination, not real. Therefore this beauty **exists** outside the mind and is something distinct from all beautiful things. In this way all ideas e.g., the idea of the horse, or beauty, or justice or goodness—are real entities. There are many horses, which are perceived by our senses, but there is only one idea horse,—as is evident from the fact that, we use one word to imply all horses. The one **ideal horse** is the **reality existing independently of all particular horses.** What then is the ultimate reality from which all else is explained? It consists, for Plato, in Ideas."

Plato explains the extra-mental reality of Ideas in another way: Our soul is immortal, it carries its knowledge of Ideas from birth to birth. Ideas of perfect straight line or perfect beauty were in the mind from our previous lives. This idea of perfection is the standard by which we can judge all perceived trianlges, straight lines or beautiful things as imperfect immitations or copies of the perfect Ideas corresponding to these. So Ideas exist independently of our minds in the realm of reality. Due to this attachment of the soul with body in this life, those ideas are now only obscure and vague. It is the aim of proper education to make the vague ideas of perfection clearer and clearer.

(a) Characteristics of Ideas

Plato now proceeds to give the characteristics of Ideas, or Forms, or Universals.

(1) Ideas exist by themselves, that's why these are called **'substances'**. Qualities depend on substances but the substance does not depend on qualities. The ideas are self-caused, self-determined, absolute and ultimate realities.

(2) Ideas are **universals**. The idea of 'cow' is not this or that particular cow. It is a general concept of all cows.

(3) Ideas are not things, but **thoughts**. Plato means by this that Ideas are not subjective ideas depending on individual minds. Ideas are objective Realities.

(4) Ideas are the **class-essences** of things and beings. Definition gives us what is common and essential in a group of particulars. 'Man' is defined as a rational animal, so that rationality is essential for all human beings. Individual men may differ in all others respects like—height, complexion, weight etc. but they must be 'rational animals.' This is implied in the idea of man.

(5) Ideas are **not in space and time,** because if they were in space and time they could have been perceived by our senses. Ideas cannot be perceived by senses, but are only known by reason.

(6) Being definitions, Ideas are permanent or unchangeable. Men may come and men may go, but the definition of 'man' remains the same. It is **eternal.**

(7) Ideas are known by thought or **reason** alone. These are not known by intuition or sense-perception. Sense perception gives us only particular things and beings. Reason gives us the Ideas.

(8) Ideas are many. There are different kinds of Ideas e.g., Ideas of class—'cat', 'man', 'horse' etc., ideas of quality like 'whiteness', 'roundness', etc., ideas of relations like 'equality', 'similarity' etc., ideas of mathematics like straight lines, dots, circles and triangles, ideas of ideals like 'truth', 'beauty' and 'goodness'. There are even the Ideas of 'filth', 'hair' etc.

(9) Though Ideas are of many kinds, they are related to each other in a system of hierarchy. The less wider Ideas are included in the wider Ideas, the wider ones in still wider ideas, thus all ideas are comprehended in one absolute idea of the Good. The ideas of redness and blueness are included in the wider idea of colour; the ideas of colour and taste, in the idea of quality. Ultimately on the top of all ideas in the pyramidal arrangement is the idea of the God, which embraces every other idea. Each idea has under it all the members of a class. The idea 'man' is one, but it is a unity of all the members of the class man. Thus an idea is **a unity in diversity**. It comprehends within itself each and every member of the same class.

Ideas reside in sense-objects. A cat is cat only because the idea of catness resides in it. It is particular, unreal but it is real in so far as it participates in the universal. There are many blue things but one 'blueness' residing in every blue thing. Blueness, catness etc. are known by our reason, blue things and cats are known by our sense-perception. All particular objects are only appearances of the Ideas, which are realities. A philosopher wants to know the truth, the ultimate reality or, in Plato's language, the Ideas or Forms. The common man wants to know the appearances only.

Plato explains the **relation of ideas among themselves** in the following way. ["The same class may be a **genus in relation to another class, and species in relation to a higher or wider class.** In this way starting from the narrowest species we may rise to higher and wider classes, and get a hierarchy of classes. Corresponding to it we get a hierarchy of universals or Ideas or reality. As we go from the lowest level gradually to the upper levels of class, the number of genus gradually diminishes, at the highest or widest stage, there will be only one class, the Summum genus. Similarly the ideas corresponding to the classes will be only one universal that exists. This highest universal is the idea of the good. All ideas come under this one Idea, the idea of the Good.] **This is how the ideas are related to each other** in Plato's philosophy. According to Plato, philosophers who want to achieve knowledge of reality knows this all-embracing organised system of Ideas, which is the unity in diversity. This system of Ideas is supersensible substances and can be known only by Reason.

In another argument Plato tries to prove the objective reality of the Ideas or universals. Ideas are created by Demiurge or Power of God, and the particular objects of this world are copies of these Ideas. Thus the Ideas are at the same time independent of the individual mind as well as independent of God's mind. This is how the objective reality of Ideas is served, by Plato.

(b) Objections Against the Objectivity of Ideas

But **Plato's arguments in favour of the objective reality of Ideas is not satisfactory,** because, firstly, he thinks that nothing in this world is perfect. We know the imperfect nature of the worldly things by the fact that there is an objective standard of perfect beauty and perfect moral action in our mind beforehand. This standard is not subjective but is real independently of all minds. But we can explain this fact without reference to objectivity of Ideas. We can judge one imperfect piece of beauty with a more perfect beauty. In this way we may reach a beautiful thing such that it is not possible for human mind to conceive of a more beautiful thing. And this is the Idea of Beauty, which we have reached by experience and not by any a priori standard of perfection.

Moreover, Plato takes recourse to pre-existence of Soul before birth, to explain the objective reality of Ideas or Forms. But this doctrine of the pre-existence of soul is only a hypothesis, not an established and verified theory.

(c) Relation of Ideas with Particular Things of the World

Regarding the relation of Ideas with particular objects of the world, Plato says that the Ideas are the cause, the ground of sense objects. Ideas reside in these objects, and the objects are not illusory. They are also real in so far as they share the universals. Plato sometimes uses the expression "copies" or 'imitations', sometimes "participation" to explain the exact relation between the particulars and the Ideas. According to him sense-objects are just dim or poor, imperfect **copies** of the universals. Again he says that things participate in the Ideas, Beautiful objects participate in one Beauty, blue objects participate in one Blueness. Thus beauty is the cause of beautiful things, blueness is the cause of blue objects. Ideas are, therefore, both transcendent and immanent. Transcendent in as much as they have real existence of their own, independently of particular things. Immanent in the sense that Ideas **reside** in the particular things.

(d) Hierarchy of Ideas

Plato thus explains in his own way the relation of one and many. One according to him involves the idea of many and cannot be thought without many. Again, 'one' can be defined only as that which is not many, and many is that which is not one. These two, one and many, are correlative ideas which involve each other. The ideas or universals, which according to Plato form a pyramid, as it were, has an apex. This highest idea is the Idea of the Good; it is the supreme Idea, the ultimate ground of itself and other Ideas and of the entire universe. This is Plato's science of Ideas or the Dialectic, or the Theory of Ideas. It is the knowledge of the relations of all the Ideas to each other, which is the goal of knowledge for philosophers.

IV. Critical Estimate of the Doctrine of Ideas

(1) Plato has made no attempt at explaining how actually all other Ideas are derived from one single Idea. There is one important drawback in the dialectic, which Plato should have remedied. Supreme idea, he says, is the Good. It is the ground of all other ideas. He ought to have derived all other Ideas from this one highest Idea. But he has not done it.

(2) Again, Plato often identified God with the supreme idea of the Good. But how is God and the Idea of the Good, related? Either God is identical with the Good, or not. If God is different from the highest idea, as Zeller points out, there are only three possibilities—(i) God is the ground of the idea of the Good. This possibility shows that the Good, as the highest Idea, is not substance, or ultimate reality. (ii) The second possibility is God owes his being to the idea of the Good. This destroys God's prestige and makes him dependent for his existence on the Idea of the Good. Then God becomes only an appearance. (iii) The third alternative is that God and the Good are equally independent ultimate realities—which means Plato's theory is nothing but dualism.

The central thesis of Plato's whole system of philosophy is the Theory of Ideas. All else—his physics, his politics his view on art—is but deduction from this theory of ideas. It is here that we must look, alike for his merits and the defects of Plato's system.

Plato's theory is that the Absolute reality is reason, is thought. This is the fundamental thesis of Idealism. Plato, therefore, is the founder of all idealism. His greatest contribution to history of philosophy is that "Absolute reality is universal thought."

As Plato has described—ideas and the particular things of this world are opposed to each other by nature. Ideas are universals, particulars are individuals, Ideas are realities, particulars are appearances. Ideas are known by reason, particulars are known by perception. Ideas are beyond space and time, particular are always spatial and temporal, Ideas are thoughts, particular are things. Ideas are self-caused, independent of particulars, but the particulars have their grounds in Ideas and are real in so far as the they participate in Ideas. The question now arises. How the Ideas or the Forms or the universals are related to the particulars? In his book "Parmenides" Plato explains the relation as (1) existing between the original and the copy. (2) Sometimes he says that the relation is of participation. Particulars are dim, imperfect copies of the Ideas. Individual men are imperfect copies of the Idea Man. Plato again says—particulars participate in the universal, the individual men participate in the Idea of 'Man'.

(1) But 'copy' or immitation is a metaphor. Similarly, 'participation' between the Idea and the particulars is also a metaphor. Metaphor is not an explanation. If the particulars are copies of the Ideas, then the universals are to be treated as particulars. The copy of a tree is particular, but the original tree also is a particular. The original and the copy—both are particulars. If both the idea and the particulars under it are treated as particulars, then on the basis of the common features between the two, we'll have to admit of another 'idea' (universal). This last idea, if taken as the original, will be a particular, to explain which we should admit of as another idea. In this way, we will have to face infinite regress.

Aristotle, the disciple of Plato, put forward a similar argument against Plato's theory, which is known as **'Third-man-argument'.** "When an individual is a copy of an idea, the individual and the idea are similar; therefore there will have to be another idea, embracing both the particulars and the original idea. And there will have to be yet another, embracing the particulars and the two idea, and so on **ad infinitum**." (B. Russell; p. 128).

Universals must not be identified, even by analogy, with any things that are particulars, for to do so would be to make them no longer universals. The relation of universals (Ideas or Forms) is not like any other relation. The relation of copy to a thing of which it is a copy, is still the relation between one particular and another.

(2) Plato used another metaphor to explain the relation between the idea and the particular thing. The particular "participaties" in the universal. The crew and the passengers of ship participate in the ship. But this analogy does not stand. Because the men in the ship, the ship itself, are both particulars. Perhaps, Plato was conscious of this problem. In 'Parmenides', Plato himself, in the words of Parmanides, raises two questions : (a) Does the individuals participate in the whole idea? or (b) Only in a part of it? If we take the first alternative then we should admit that one idea is equally and totally present in each and every individual member of a class. If the second alternative is accepted then the idea is one and many at the same time. But each goes against Plato's theory of Ideas.

The relation may be explained as follows. The relation cannot be literally or even similar to any of the situation that Plato presents. As John Hospers observes: "A more accurate statement of the relation, at which Plato hinted but never fully stated, would be: **The relation between the (Ideas) universals and particulars is like no other relation.** It is the relation of exemplification of instancing, which is uniquely different from any other relation that there is. A particular blue instances or exemplifies blueness, this triangle instances triangularity and so on." (p. 357).

Following Thilly we may conclude by saying that with the possible exception of Plato's theory of forms, no other Platonic theory (e.g., his doctrine of soul, God, world, his philosophy of Politics, Ethics and Nature) has exerted a longer or more continuous influence. "Plato's doctrine of ideas, though it contains a number of errors, yet, it marks a very important advance in philosophy, since it is the first theory to emphasise the problem of universals, which has persisted to the present day. We cannot express ourselves in a language composed wholly of proper names, but must have also general words such as "man", "dog", "cat", or relational words like 'similar', 'before' and so on. Such words are not meaningless noises and it is difficult to see how they can have meaning if the world consists entirely of particular things, such as is designated by proper names. Plato's theory of forms or ideas affords a prima facie case in favour of universals (B. Russell). He failed to realise how great is the gap between universals and particulars. His 'ideas' are just other particulars. He himself, at a later date, began to see this difficulty, as appears in Parmenides, which contains, according to B. Russell, one of the most remarkable cases in history of **self-criticism by a philosopher**.

As W. T. Stace observes, any successful philosophy must satisfy two conditions: (1) It must be capable of explaining the world, and (2) It must explain its first principle as self-explanatory.

Regarding explanation of the world, Plato says that the world of particular things and beings are "copies" or 'imitation' of the Ideas. They "participate" in the Ideas. But why? Why do such copies exist? There must be reason for it. This reason must exist in the nature of the Ideas themselves. There must be an inner necessity in the Ideas which force them to reproduce themselves in things. But there is no such necessity in Plato's Ideas. The Ideas are sole reality. They are self-sufficient. They lack nothing. It is not necessary for them to achieve anything. There are white objects in the world. But why should the Idea of whiteness produce white things? There is in the Ideas no necessity forcing them towards reproduction of themselves. Thus we can say that they possess no principle for the explanation of things.

The second test is whether the principle of Ideas is a self-explanatory principle. Now the only self-explanatory principle in the world is reason itself. Reason is its own reason. Explanation of a thing means showing that the thing is rational. When Plato says that the Absolute is concept, he says that it is reason. Merit of Plato lies in this recognition of the final principle of his philosophy as reason or concept. But, to be self-explanatory, each concept must be a necessary concept. But Plato's Ideas are not of this necessary kind. We can think the world without the idea of whiteness. Why is there an Idea of whiteness? We cannot see. There is no reason. There is no necessity. The same thing applies to all other ideas. They are not rational concepts.

Plato says that the ultimate ground or reason of all lower ideas will be found in the Supreme idea of the Good. But it is not possible to deduce the idea of whiteness from the idea of the Good. It is quite possible to think the Good without thinking of whiteness.

Plato takes the universal as a particular, when he says that particulars are copies or imitations of them. But to form a picture of the universal is to think it just what it is not, an individual.

Thus the Ideas of Plato cannot explain their relation to the world nor can the Ideas explain themselves. Plato's Ideas exist in a world of their own. So, Stace comments that "Plato commits the greatest sin that can be ascribed to a philosopher. He treats thought as a thing. He was the great founder of Idealism, but his idealism is crude."

Aristotle

(384 B.C.-322 B.C.)

2

CHAPTER

. Life and Writings

Aristotle was born in 384 B.C. at Stagyra, in Greece. His father Nicomachus was amily physician of the King of Macedon. He came to Athens at the age of 17, joined Plato's Academy, and became a pupil of Plato. He remained in the Academy for wenty years, until the death of Plato in 348-7 B.C. He became tutor of Alexander, the son of the King of Macedon. This son is the famous Alexander the Great.

Aristotle studied philosophy as well as different branches of natural sciences. In act, he had a keen interest in the world of experience and is the founder of at least wo sciences : (1) Logic and (2) Biology. It was during his long stay in Athens, That he founded his school and wrote most of his books. After the death (323 B.C.) of Alexander, the Athenians rebelled, and Aristotle had to flee to avoid punishment in 323 B.C. In the next year (322 B.C.) he died.

Aristotle's treatises are systemic, his discussions are divided into heads, critical nd he is a professional teacher. There is no branch of knowledge which did not eceive his attention. He was very fond of physical science. Where there was no cience, his plan involved the foundation of new sciences. He wrote on Logic and Metaphysics, upon Ethics, Politics and Art, on Astronomy, and Meteorology and on Biology. He criticised Plato's views on Metaphysics, yet he was the greatest of all Platonists, because his philosophy is founded upon the Idea, and is an attempt to ound an idealism free from the defects of Plato's system. He saw for the first time that art and science each have their own sphere. If we desire truth, we must stick to eason, and avoid poetic metaphors.

'Aristotle's system of philosophy falls into the fivefold division of Logic, metaphysics, physics, ethics and aesthetics.' We'll discuss in details only his metaphysics here.

II. Aristotle's Metaphysics

Aristotle's metaphysics was called "First Philosophy" by Aristotle himself, for it was an attempt to know the first, the highest, and the most general principle of the universe. All other sciences deal with less universal principles and are dependent on this study of knowledge for the sake of knowledge. Andronicus published a complete edition of Aristotle's known works. The treatise on "first philosophy" was placed in this edition, after the "physics", and metaphysics signifies beyond or "after physics". Metaphysics is, according to Aristotle, wisdom par excellence, and the philosopher or lover of wisdom is he who desires knowledge about that ultimate cause and nature of Reality and desires that knowledge—for its own sake.

Aristotle began his metaphysical discussions mainly by criticising Plato's theory of Ideas or Forms. In fact, Aristotle wanted to overcome the defects which he found in Plato's philosophy, to criticise them, to reject what was useless in it, to retain the residue of truth and to add to it his own suggestions and original ideas.

The main points of Aristotle's criticism against Plato's doctrine of Ideas or Forms are:

(1) Plato's Ideas cannot explain how particular things exist. If universals can exist without the particulars, then how they are related to each other remains unexplained. But the main problem of philosophy is to explain why the world is. Plato's theory of Ideas fails to explain this.

(2) The question "How the Ideas are related to the world of things"? has not been answered by Plato. He tries to explain the relation with the help of some metaphors. According to Plato, particular things are 'copies' of the Ideas, or particulars 'participate' in the universals. But these metaphors also are not appropriate in the sense that if particulars are 'copies' of the Ideas, then, like the relation of all copies and originals, the tree and its copy on the paper, the universals' become particulars.

(3) The world is a world of change, motion, life, becoming. This motion, growth and decay which are characteristic of this world of particular things cannot be explained by the universals or the Ideas. The idea of beauty may produce the beautiful things, idea of whiteness may produce white things, but, as Plato thinks, ideas are themselves immutable and motionless—so the world, which is the 'copy' of the Ideas, would be motionless or static, and lifeless.

(4) Aristotle criticised Plato's attempt to explain the relation between Ideas and particular things of the world by saying that 'Plato is like a man who, being unable to count with a small number, imagines, if he doubles the number, he will be able to count more easily'. 'Ideas are nothing but externalised things of nature'—Prof. Stace observes.

(5) According to Plato, wherever there is a common element, there must be an Idea. John, Smith, Jack and Robin are 'men' because they have the common element 'man-ness' in them, or the Idea of man, in them. "But there is also an element common

to the individual man and to the Idea of man. There must, therefore, be a further Idea, the "third man", to explain this. And, between this further Idea and the individual man, there must be yet another Idea, to explain what they have in common, and so on "ad infinitum". According to B. Russell, this argument against Plato is the strongest of all arguments.

(6) But the most important of all Aristotle's objections to Plato's theory of Ideas is that it assumes that Ideas are the essences of things and yet exists not in them, but outside them, in a mysterious world of their own. The universal 'horse' is the reality of all 'individual horses' and must be found in the particulars. But Plato thinks that besides the individual horses, which we know, there is another individual horse-in-general. Besides white-things, there is a thing called 'Whiteness'. According to Aristotle, universal is the reality of the particulars, it cannot exist independently of the particulars. The universals, if they exist, exist in and through the particulars.

The fundamental principle of Aristotle's philosophy is that universals are the only realities but they exist only in the particulars. The first question of philosophy is: What is reality? What is substance? A substance has an independent existence of its own. It does not depend for its existence on anything else. A substance is the reality. It is never a predicate, it is that on which predicates are applied. "Gold is heavy." Here gold is the subject or substance, and 'heavy' is the predicate. Heaviness depends for its existence on the gold—which is the substance. Thus Plato's universals are not substances. Universal is common predicate which attaches to many objects of a class. Idea of man is what is common to all men. It is 'man-ness', a predicate, which cannot exist without human beings or men. So universals are not substances.

But the particulars also are not substances. If 'man-ness' does not exist without 'man', similarly 'man' does not exist without man-ness. Gold cannot exist without its qualities, as the qualities of gold like heaviness, yellowness etc. cannot exist apart from the gold. Thus gold depends as much on its qualities, as the qualities of gold depend on the gold. So, neither of them is substance or reality. Neither of them can exist without the other. A substance must be a compound of the two; it must be the universal in the particular. Thus the individual objects alone are the substances, e.g., gold with all its qualities attached to it.

Aristotle is against Plato when he denies that the universal can exist independently of the particulars, but he agrees with Plato that the universal is the real. When Aristotle says that the universal is not substance, he means, as against Plato, that it is existent. But universal is real, though not existent. As B. Russell observes: "This much may be taken as proved, but Aristotle's own doctrine is far from clear. It was this lack of clarity that made possible the medieval controversy between nominalists and realists."[1]

III. Aristotle's Doctrine of Causation

The metaphysical problem here is, for Aristotle, the problem of change. The things and beings of this world are always changing. We, the ordinary people, think that each change has some cause behind it. 'The cause is merely the mechanism by which

[1] See Locke's Conceptualism

a reason produces its consequence. There is a distinction between a cause and a reason. Death is caused by poison, or accident or disease. But these causes cannot explain why death should be in the world at all. A philosopher wants to know the reason behind an occurrence. Modern science gives us a mechanical view of the universe, and, therefore, considers only mechanical causes. But Aristotle's theory, being philosophical, gives an wider conception of cause which includes both the principles of mechanism and teleology.

In this wide sense Aristotle finds that there are **four kinds of causes : the material, the efficient, the formal, and the final cause.** In every case, in the occurrence of any event or existence of any thing, all the four causes operate simultaneously. The same four causes are to be found both in human and natural productions.

(1) **The material cause** of a thing like a bronze statue of Mahatma Gandhi—the bronze is the material cause of the statue. Here bronze is a kind of matter or material object.

(2) **The efficient cause** is always defined by Aristotle as the cause of motion. It is the force or energy required to produce change. When a leaf changes its colour from green to yellow, it is an instance of motion, just as a falling stone is an instance of motion. This efficient cause is the cause of all change. It causes the bronze to become a statue. **The sculptor** produces the change, so the sculptor is the efficient cause of the bronze statue.

(3) **The formal cause** is the essence of a thing—says Aristotle. It is the concept or Idea of the thing. **The idea of the statue** in the mind of the sculptor is the formal cause. Thus we see that Plato's Idea comes back in Aristotle as formal cause.

(4) The **final cause** is the end or purpose or aim towards which the movement is directed, i.e., **the completed statue** itself, which the sculptor aims.

Thus Aristotle's conception of cause is much wider than the modern scientific conception of it. The scientific definition of cause, as we find it in Mill's definition, is, "a cause is the immediate, unconditional invariable antecedent of a phenomenon." Here there is no reference to final causes because final cause is the end, and is not an antecedent in time. There is no mention of formal cause also. Only material and efficient causes remain, that means only material and efficient causes are considered as causes, which are actually the modern notions of matter and energy. In fact, modern science does not deny formal and final causes. It only considers them to be outside the sphere of science. Formal and material causes are actually the reasons of an event, is the answer to the question: why the event occurs, or why the thing exists? Science takes it for granted that things exist, and they give only a mechanical view of causation.

IV. Aristotle's Doctrine of Form and Matter

Aristotle's theory of Form and Matter is nothing but the reduction of these four principles to two, which he calls matter and form. He shows that formal cause, efficient cause, and final cause—all melt into the single conception of Form.

The formal cause and the final cause are the same, because formal cause is the essence, the Idea of the thing. The final cause is the end, and is only the actualisation of the Idea.

The efficient cause is the same as final cause, because of the efficient cause is the cause of becoming and what causes the becoming is just that it aims at the end e.g., the end, or the final cause of an acorn is the oak. And it is the oak that causes the acorn's growth. The efficient cause of the statue is the sculptor, but the idea of the completed statue moves him to act on the brass. Here the same is conscious.

Thus Matter and Form are the two fundamental categories of Aristotle's philosophy. Now we may try to explain and understand their **Characteristics.**

Firstly, matter and form are inseparable. We may separate them in thought, but in fact, they are inseparable. There cannot be form without matter or matter without form. No such thing exists. According to Aristotle, Plato was wrong in thinking that Form or Idea exists in a supersensible world of its own.

Secondly, form is the universal and matter is the particular. Universals, according to Aristotle, exists only in particulars. Every individual is a compound of matter and form, and every individual is a compound of universal and particular. Individual things exist, but particulars cannot exist without the universals.

For Aristotle, matter is a relative conception in the sense that what is matter in relation to something may be form in relation to something else. Wood is form in relation to the growing plant, which is matter in relation to oak furniture. That is form towards which the change operates.

Similarly, **shape and form are not the same**. Shape is always the shape. Form includes organisation. Form is not merely shape. 'For, the hand cut off does not lose its shape.'

Thirdly, Form includes all the qualities of a thing. Matter is what has these qualities. A thing cannot exist without qualities, just as qualities cannot exist without things.

Fourthly, the matter is absolutely formless. In itself it has no qualities. It may become anything according to the form impressed on it. Thus matter is the possibility of everything, though it is actually nothing.

"Here Aristotle distinguishes between **potentiality** and **actuality.** Potentiality is matter and actuality is form. Relation between the oak seed and the oak tree is the relation of possibility and actuality. The seed is the potential oak tree, and the oak tree is the actuality of the seed. Again, the oak furniture is actuality with reference to the oak tree which is now potentiality. Thus the relation between the principle of potentiality and the principle of actuality is similar to the relation between form and matter, Aristotle calls matter as potentiality and form as actuality. All the objects of this world are compounds of these two—form and matter, actuality and potentiality."

There are only two exceptions, to this general rule, viz, the lowest state of pure matter, and the highest state of pure form—which Aristotle calls "the concept of God".

According to Aristotle, though form and matter are two fundamental categories, form is ideationally prior to and higher than matter. He claims that by means of the antithesis of potentiality and actuality, he has solved the ancient problem of becoming, which troubled almost all great thinkers of Greece. **Potentiality and actuality are not absolute terms, these are relative terms,** which shade off into each other. Becoming, or change, or motion is the passage of potentiality into actuality, of matter into form. It is not a leap from nothing to something. What matter is to become, is already present in it ideally and potentially, though not actually. The **end,** therefore, is already present in the beginning. The oak is in the acorn ideally. Thus end is the operative principle or the cause of true becoming. Motion is not pushing from behind, but drawing the thing towards its end. The end, which is a principle of form, is, thus, the absolute first in thought and, reality, though last in time.

V. Aristotle's Theory of God

The world-process is a continual elevation of matter into higher and higher forms. At the bottom lies the formers matter, at the top absolutely matterless form. Both of these are abstractions.

The highest and **absolute form** is called by Aristotle **God**. God alone is **real**. He is absolutely **actual**, because he is pure form.

The principle of form includes the formal, the final and the efficient causes—God is all these. As **formal cause** He is the Idea, He is essentially thought, reason. As final cause He is the absolute end. He is that towards which all beings strive. God is absolute perfection. Lastly, as **efficient cause**, God is the ultimate cause of all becoming. He is the first mover. But he is himself unmoved.

Aristotle's argument for this **unmoved mover** is this : God is absolute form. He cannot pass into any higher form, and is, therefore, unmoved. Aristotle claims, unless we so conceive it, God as the mover of all changes, remaining Himself unchanged,—no cause of motion appears. A moving object is moved by another moving object. The motion of the latter demands a further cause. In this way we are involved in "infinite regress". So the real and ultimate cause must be unmoved.

God is thought. But the thought of what? God is absolute form, so **He is form of form.** Form is universal. Universal is idea or thought. Aristotle gives us the famous definition of God, as thought of thought. God thinks thought. He is self-conscious.

The very word 'God', as Stace observes, used by Aristotle, leads us towards the idea of personality. But personality implies an individual and existent consciousness. God being absolute form, and form being universal—without particular, cannot be individual. God of Aristotle is not an individual God.

Again, God is form without matter, so He cannot be existent, though He is absolutely real. A personal God must exist. So Aristotle's God is not a personal God. It is the Absolute.

God is thought, but not subjective thought of this or that particular mind. This thought is objective, real on its own account. Plato claimed that absolute thought is real and objective, and, therefore, it exists. Aristotle avoids this error and says that Absolute thought is absolutely real, but it does not exist.

VI. Critical Comments on Aristotle's Philosophy

Here ends Aristotle's metaphysics "Aristotle's philosophy is the same as Plato's with some of the crudities and defects removed. Plato was the founder of Idealism. But he confused reality with existence, and degraded universal to a mere particular. Aristotle tried to remove this fundamental defect of Plato and make his philosophy as reasonable as possible".

Both Aristotle and Plato thought that Idea or Form or universal is the ultimate reality. But Plato thought that Ideas exist, in a world of their own. The merit of Aristotle lies in the fact that, for Aristotle, universal, though real, has no existence in a world of its own but only in this world, as a **formative principle** of particular things. Thus Aristotle's philosophy is the most perfect form of Greek Idealism.

Moreover, Aristotle deserves the credit of introducing, for the first time, a philosophy of evolution, which has a lasting influence on his successors, Hegel (1770-1831) the German philosopher of modern age, is influenced by the philosophy of evolution. This problem of becoming was a great problem for almost all Greek philosophers. What does 'becoming' mean? This was a very interesting problem for philosophers of all times. Aristotle showed that 'becoming' signifies that the world process is a rationally ordered development towards a rational end.

But the defect which we saw in Plato's philosophy is also inherent in Aristotle. Plato was unable to solve the dualism of universal and particular. Aristotle tried to remove the dualism by saying that the universal and the particular are inseparable. Thus Aristotle admitted Plato's dualism and refuted it. Aristotle showed that the universal and particular form and matter always go together—the reality is the individual—in which universal and particular, form and matter, combine together to exist in space and time. "But Aristotle was not able to deduce logically 'matter' from 'Form', as Plato was unable to deduce the particular from the universal. The dualism, thus, is neither resolved nor overcome by Aristotle."

Rene Descartes
(1596-1650)

3
CHAPTER

I. Life and Writings

Rene Descartes was born in 1596 in a small town in France, in an aristocratic family. He was educated at the Jesuit College of La Fieche for eight years. He was very much interested in Mathematics. Later he studied in Paris also for a few years. He enlisted his name in Dutch Army in 1618. As Holland was at peace, at that time, he seems to have enjoyed two years of undisturbed meditation there. In 1619 he again joined in army. In 1621 he gave up fighting and settled in Holland. He lived there for twenty years, and was working on philosophy, undisturbed. Unfortunately, Descartes got into correspondence with Queen Christina of Sweden. Descarte's writings led her to request his presence at her court. Descartes agreed. She wanted lessons from him at five in the morning three times a week. In the cold of a Scandinavian winter, Descartes fell ill and died in February 1650.

His main writings include "Discourse on Method" (Published in 1637). In 1644 "Principles of Philosophy" and in 1641 his famous writing "Meditations on First Philosophy" were published.

He never married. He was a sincere and faithful Catholic.

II. Descartes as the Father of Modern Philosophy

Descartes may truly be called the **Father of Modern Philosophy.** He was a philosopher, a mathematician, and a man of science. He invented coordinate geometry, applied algebra to geometry. He regarded bodies of man and animals as machines, but human soul is something very different in quality, from body. In fact, his interest in Mathematics and natural sciences were no less keen than his interest in philosophy.

- The outlook of modern philosophy is scientific and critical, and Descartes, being a mathematician, was thoroughly fit to be a modern philosopher.

Descartes was dissatisfied with the Scholastic philosophers and wanted completely to break with the past and to begin from the very beginning. Bacon, the British philosopher, also showed this revolting attitude. But while Bacon stopped short after giving only a programme of knowledge and merely a method of investigation, Descartes attempted to construct a real system of philosophy. Bacon was an Empicist, and took the path of Induction. But Descartes thought that the empirical and scientific way of thinking is inadequate for a comprehensive knowledge of life and reality. Descartes agreed with the natural scientists of his days, in their mechanical conception of the external world arrived at by empirical mode of investigation. But he could not dispense with the notions of God, soul and freedom, as supplied by reason, and his problem was to reconcile the discoveries of the material sciences with the principles of the Idealistic and Spiritualistic Philosophy of the past.

(a) Characteristics of Modern Philosophy

"Modern period of history has a special outlook, which differs from the medieval period in many ways. Of these, two are the most important : (i) The diminishing authority of the church, and (ii) The increasing authority of science." In Descartes, we find these attitudes in a very significant way. During medieval period, education was totally under the authority of the churches. All thinking was influenced by religion. Nobody was allowed to think against religious creeds. Freedom of thought, criticism of older views, attempt to solve different problems of life from a new point of view was not allowed. Priests were the teachers, universities ran under the supervision of the churches. All philosophical thinking centred round Aristotle's philosophy.

With the lapse of time, this situation changed. With Renaissance began a new life in European thought and culture. Scientists like Copernicus, Galileo, Kepler changed the outlook of common men as well as the educated people. Gradually the influence of religion and church diminished. Descartes was not only influenced by this changing outlook, he himself regulated the course of philosophy and general thinking of his days. He himself never accepted anything without criticism.

The medieval philosophers never cared to adopt a definite method to discuss philosophical problems. Descartes, for the first time, **applied a definite method**. All philosophers after Descartes agreed with Descartes in using a rational method to achieve the goal which philosophy wants to reach.

Before Descartes, philosophical outlook was primarily objective in the sense that, for the philosophers, reality did not depend on human mind for its existence. It was independent of knowledge. It was Descartes who for the first time told that **the world is an object of knowledge only for the subject who knows.** Descartes discussed the relation of the knower with the known, nature of knowledge, the criterion of truth, etc. As a result there grew up a new branch of philosophy called 'Epistemology'.

"Emancipation from the authority of the church led to the growth of individualism. Modern philosophy has retained for the most part an individualistic and subjective character. This is very marked in Descartes, who built up all knowledge from the certainty of his own existence and accepts clearness and distinctness (both subjective) as criterion of truth. Descartes is the first philosopher who **introduced in philosophy the concept of a 'criterion of Truth.**"

Descartes was very fond of Mathematics. He found in the mathematical method an ideal method for philosophy. The conclusion of mathematics is always certain. According to Descartes, philosophy also will achieve certain conclusions if it follows the mathematical method.

He gave philosophy a systematic and coherent form, discussing all its problems separately and clearly, with the help of a definite method of its own. He dealt with the problems of God, soul, freedom, mind-body relation, substance, quality etc. He reached his first principle—Cogito, ergo sum—which is known as "Descartes' Cogito", and the process by which he got it is known as Cartesian Doubt.

"I think, therefore I am" makes mind more certain than matter, and my mind more certain than other minds. Thus from Descartes arose **a tendency towards subjectivism**. Continental idealism proves this tendency triumphantly later.

Renaissance and new discoveries of science challenged the medieval philosophy. Discovery of steam, electricity, etc. made man confident about his power over nature. Descartes explained the external material world mechanically as was done by the scientists of his days. But he could not completely dispense with the ideas of God, soul etc. derived from reason. He tried to reconcile these ideas with the scientific discoveries based on experience and experiment. Thus from him as a common source, there sprang two main lines of modern thought—**the idealistic and the materialistic**, that play conspicuous part in the history of modern philosophy. In this sense, Descartes may properly be called "the father of modern philosophy".

III. Descartes on the Method of Philosophy

Descartes was a great mathematician. His problem was to secure the same amount of certainity in philosophy as we find in Mathematics. He thought that this could be achieved if the method of philosophical investigation be modelled after the fashion of mathematical method. In mathematics we start with simple fundamental ideas and axioms that are self-evident, certain, intuitively arrived at; and then deduce consequences from them. The two steps involved in mathematical reasoning are intuition and deduction.

The same method is to be applied in philosophy. We should proceed from absolutely certain first principle, from propositions which are clear and self-evident and pass on to new and unknown truths which are equally certain. But how to get such fundamental self-evident truths? The traditional Scholastic system cannot provide us with such truths for we find in them only a bundle of divergent opinions. As Prof. Thilly observes, There is not a single subject in philosophy that is not still being disputed.

"Moreover we should not accept any truth on the authority of others. We must judge by ourselves and receive nothing as true which we do not clearly and definitely perceive to be true. Thus to arrive at truths which are self-evident and certain Descartes employed the method of scepticism—His starting point is "Universal methodic doubt."—known as Cartesian Doubt. i.e., doubt which consists in doubting everything till that doubt itself implies something which cannot be further doubted. "As for the opinions which up to that time I had embraced; I thought them I could not do better than resolve at once to sweep them wholly away, that I might afterwards be in a position to admit either others more correct, or even perhaps the same when they had undergone the scrutiny of reason." Descartes tells us in this context that by **'method' is meant a set of rules, by following which we can avoid all false knowledge and attain certainty**. Following these rules depend on two fundamental mental activities—intuition and deduction.

By **intuition** Descartes meant direct perception by reason independently of any sense experience. It is so clear and distinct that we can never doubt it. Descartes is marked as a Rationalist because he considered reason as the only source of knowledge. By **deduction** Descartes meant that mental process with the help of which unknown and less certain truths are deduced in such a way from self-evident truths that these can also be treated as self-evident and certain.

Descartes doubted not merely the principles laid down by tradition and authority but also the reality of sensations for these often deceive us. We cannot be certain even of our own bodies and actions, for of these also we may be deceived e.g., in dreams, when we believe we have reality before us, whereas they are nothing but illusions. Descartes doubts in the beginning even the truths of Geometry and Mathematics. As Descartes himself says in his 'Discourse on Method', "... I reject as absolutely false everything concerning which I could imagine the least ground of doubt, in order to see whether afterwards there remained anything in my belief which was certainly certain".

Thus Descartes asks to start "de novo" with an unprejudiced mind free from all pre-suppositions on the path of philosophical enquiry. He framed **certain rules to apply his method successfully**. These are:

(1) Do not receive anything as a truth which you do not clearly know to be such. As Copleston observes, "observance of this precept involves the use of methodic doubt".

(2) Divide every difficulty into as many parts as possible.

(3) Conduct your thought in an orderly manner beginning with objects, the most simple and the easiest to understand, in order to ascend by steps to the knowledge of the most composite.

(4) Make enumeration so complete and review so comprehensive that you may be certain of committing no error.

Following these four rules implies not to accept anything as true without criticism.

Descartes is not a thoroughgoing sceptic. He doubts not merely for the sake of doubting, but he doubts all these only to re-admit them, if they stand the test of reason. Descarte's scepticism may be called "**Provisional Scepticism**—a temporary suspense of judgment as long as there is no clear evidence for taking a final decision."

As Copleston remarks: "It (doubt) is methodic in the sense that it is practiced not for the sake of doubting but as a preliminary stage in the attainment of certainty and in shifting the true from the false, the certain from the probable, the indubitable from the doubtful." R. Falkenberg also comments "It (Descartes' doubt) is precept, not doctrine, the starting point of philosophy, not its conclusion". Descartes' doubt is provisional, and hypothetical not final.

IV. Cogito, ergo sum or Descartes' First Principle

The truth, which Descartes discovers to be beyond all possibilities of doubt, is the fact of his own conscious thought. When everything else has been doubted, there is one thing beyond the reach of doubt, which in the very process of doubting I tacitly affirm. I cannot doubt the doubter. Doubt is thought and in thinking I cannot but affirm the existence of the thinker. Thought without a thinker is an impossible conception. The more I doubt, the more clearly and indubilably conscious be I of myself existing as a thinking being. "Cogito, ergo sum"—I think, therefore I exist. In the very act of thinking I have an inmediate intuition of the unity of thought and being. This intuition of thought and being as identical is the starting point of Descartes' whole system.

From this certitude of the self Descartes proceeds to reestablish the world of mind and matter which he had doubted away in the beginning. This intuition furnishes Descartes also with the test or criterion by which the validity of other truths is to be measured. For, Descartes thinks that whatever has the same amount of certainty (clearness and distinctness) as this cogito, ergo sum, may be taken as demonstrated.

Gassendi, a contemporary of Descartes, argues that one may as well infer existence from any other action, such as walking, eating etc. as from thinking. To this Descartes replies that existence cannot be inferred from walking or from any other action, for the certainty of our walking or eating depends upon our thinking, i.e., being conscious of it. Besides we may be deceived as to walking etc., as in dreams, but of thinking there cannot be any doubt, for we think even when we doubt.

Saint Augustine advanced an argument closely similar to the cogito. But he had not given prominence to it. Descartes' originality lies in perceiving its importance.

Descartes' "Cogito, ergo sum" must not be taken as an inference with the major premise "All thinking beings exist." For, as Descartes himself admits, that would be only begging the question. "Cogito, ergo sum" is an inference only in appearance, it is simply an analytic judgement or a self-evident proposition. What we start from is the particular immediate consciousness that, in my thought, existence is implied.

Having now secured a firm foundation, Descartes sets to work to rebuild the edifice of knowledge.

Implications of 'Cogito, ergo sum'

The **first implication** of the principle is that **thinking is the primary quality of mind or self.** We can never think of mind except as thinking. All other qualities may be denied of it, but the mind would cease to exist if it ceases to think.

The next implication is that cogito is so evident because it is clear and distinct. He, therefore, adopts as a general rule the principle : **All things that we conceive very clearly and very distinctly are true.** The clearness and distinctness of Descartes' principle makes one absolutely unable to doubt it and Descartes takes this clearness and distinctness as the test or criterion of truth.

But to this criterion of clearness and distinctness the objection may be raised that all ideas which we believe to be true seem clear to us. The qualities of clearness and distinctness admit of degrees and may vary with individual minds. Descartes tries to overcome this objection by drawing a distinction between a natural inclination—impelling one to believe in a thing that nevertheless may be false, and a natural light—which makes one **know** that it is true. But Descartes' conception of natural light is very vague and he never explains it fully.

The **third implication** is that Descartes uses the word "Thinking" in a very wide sense. A thinking being is one that doubts, understands, conceives, affirms, denies, wills, imagines and feels.

The fourth implication

This principle is such that it makes mind **more certain than matter** and my mind more certain than the mind of others. Thus, from Descartes, we find in all philosophy a subjective tendency to establish the knowledge of matter as dependent on the knowledge of mind.

Not only Idealistic philosophy, but contemporary and later empiricism also have been influenced by this outlook of Descartes. Locke, Berkeley, Hume and other philosophers took this subjective outlook in epistemology and proved that mind can know directly only its own ideas, the knowledge of the external world is only indirect, through these ideas. Herein lies the importance of Descartes' first principle.

The fifth implication

Moreover, there is another important truth implied in the principle, Cogito, ergo sum. Matter and mind, self and not-self, knower and the known—these are not identical. These are basically different. Descartes' principle proves the reality of the self or soul, or the knower, but the external world or non-self matter remains unproved. Thus there is a dualism inherent in Descartes' principle, and Descartes is known in the history of philosophy as a dualist.

Criticism

Copleston criticises Descartes' Cogito, ergo sum by saying that he had no justification for asserting that I am a thing which thinks. He only assumes uncritically the scholastic notion of substance which the doctrine ought really to have been subjected to the test of doubt.

But this criticism is not acceptable because Descartes' principle is not a sum-total of two separate realisations like 'I think' and 'I am', In fact "Cogito, ergo sum" is a synthetic a priori proposition in the sense that it is a complete and comprehensive truth which cannot be analysed into parts. It is direct perception of the existence of self as a thinking being, and is necessarily true adding newness to knowledge—a synthetic a priori proposition.

Descartes, thus, is unable to prove the reality of the external world directly. He has proved the reality of the thinking subject as independent of the known object. So the dualism of matter and mind, self and not-self is inevitable for him. In fact, he deduced much less from his principle than he could have deduced. The German philosopher Hegel and his followers claimed that Descartes could have proved the reality of the external world also from his principle, Cogito, ergo sum, as, the thought process implies not only the thinker but also the thought object. The object of thinking is equally important as the subject, and is equally necessary for thinking. Descartes proved only the subject. That is why dualism creeps in his philosophy.

V. Descartes' Explanation of the External World

Now, Descartes proceeds to prove the reality of the world. But he cannot prove it directly from Cogito. First he proves the existence of the Supreme Mind or God, then, indirectly, from God he proceeds to prove the existence of the external world.

The self has been demonstrated to be existing as certain. Now Descartes has to reestablish the reality of those things which he had doubted away in the beginning, for otherwise his position would be extremely solipsistic, the self being confined within its own limits. But Descartes would not proceed to prove the reality of the extra-mental world directly, because, the self has been proved to be existing as a thinking substance even when all other things have been denied. The dualism of mind and matter—which had a far reaching influence in the subsequent history of philosophy—follows thus from Descartes' abstract conception of self. Descartes had proved too little from his principle "Cogito, ergo sum", for, as Hegel pointed out later—thought necessarily implies a subject which thinks and an object which is thought of, and thus the reality of both the subject and the object follows from "I think" whereas Descartes only asserts the reality of the subject in abstraction from the object.

Whatever that may be, the way which Descartes follows is first to prove the existence of God and then indirectly to prove the existence of the extramental world.

Descartes is neither a solipsist, nor a subjective Idealist. He takes recourse to his first principle, in order to explain the world of things and beings, of God's existence. His Cogito, ergo sum, supplied him with a criterion of truth. Why is 'Cogito, ergo sum' self-evident? Descartes' answer is, because it is clear and distinct. That I exist is an indubitable truth. Everything else can be doubted but the clearness and distinctness with which we perceive ourselves as existing cannot be denied. Descartes claims that the clearness and distinctness with which I know myself is the criterion of truth. Whatever has the same amount of certainty (clearness and distinctness) as this 'Cogito, ergo sum' may be taken as demonstrated.

VI. Descartes' Theory of Ideas

We find a great numbers of ideas in our mind. Descartes classifies these ideas under three heads:

(1) There are the adventitious ideas. These ideas seem to come in our minds from outside, but we can never be sure of these ideas for they may be the results of dreams or illusions. We get these ideas through our sense-organs. Colour, taste, smell, tree, river, mountain, all these are adventitious ideas—and are not at all clear and distinct. So these do not give us knowledge proper.

(2) We have factitious ideas. These ideas are of our own inventions and no question of the reality or certitude of them arises, e.g., the ideas of unicorn, a winged horse, or a fairy. These are often based on adventitious ideas. So we never get knowledge with the help of factitious ideas.

(3) Thirdly, we have what Descartes called **the "Innate Ideas"**. These are ideas which the mind necessarily thinks in being conscious of itself. As such ideas are derived from reason, their denial leads us to self-contradiction. The law of Identity, in Logic, is an innate idea. It is a universal principle, and, therefore, not derived from sense-experience. It is independent of sense-perception and is clear and distinct e.g., the knowledge that if A is A, then it is always A. From such clear and distinct innate ideas it is possible to deduce other ideas and get certain knowledge. Innate ideas are neither the result of external impressions nor the products of imagination. These are in the mind since our birth and our mind simply unfolds them afterwards. He mentions the idea of God, axioms of arithmetic, Laws of thought, out of nothing, nothing comes or the idea of ex nihilo, nihil fit etc. as examples of Innate ideas.

[We may notice in this connection that though Descartes takes these ideas as a priori, he maintains that experience is needed to make them clear. These are not clear and distinct from the time of birth. As Copleston puts it "Descartes' theory would thus constitute, to some extent, an anticipation of Kant's theory of the a priori".]

There are two main characteristics of Innate ideas according to Descartes: (1) These are universally present in all minds. (2) and are uniformly present. His argument to prove the **universality of the idea** of 'perfection' is that every man knows himself as imperfect. This shows that he has, within his mind, the idea of perfection, by contrasting with which, he knows himself to be an imperfect being. So the idea is **universal** and **innate**.

Again the idea of perfection is uniform in the sense that it cannot vary from individual to individual. It is always the same. There is no difference of degree in this idea. It is one idea and only one.

The British Empiricist Locke criticised Descartes' theory of Innate Ideas, and said 'mind is a tabula rasa' (Tabula rasa—clean slate, pure uninfluenced mind) at the time of birth. But Descartes never said that Innate ideas are in the mind in a fullfledged form. He specifically mentioned that mind has a tendency to form such ideas but it requires adequate and suitable situation to make them explicit. Descartes never intended to imply that infants in the womb have an actual notion of God, but only that there is in us by nature an innate potentiality whereby we know God—says Copleston.

Idea of God as an Innate Idea

Descartes deduces the existence of God as a most perfect being, to avoid solipism. Cogito, ergo sum proves conclusively that I exist and thought is my essence. To prove the existence of other minds and the world outside is a problem for Descartes. That is why he proves the existence of God from his own existence.

As Descartes observes, among the innate ideas there is the idea of the infinite and all-perfect being, and this is the most important and fundamental of all ideas. In being conscious of ourselves we are conscious of our finitude and relatedness and we cannot be conscious of these without thinking that they are co-related to the infinite and the absolute. This is the idea of God in us. By God Desceates understands "a substance omniscient, infinite, eternal, immutable, independent, omnipotent, by whom myself and all other things have been created".

VII. Proofs for the Existence of God

Descartes examined the source and implications of this idea of God and advances **the famous proofs for the existence of God** in course of examination. **There are three arguments** of which two are causal, while the third argument is metaphysical or a priori. (1) The **first causal argument** is : It is a self-evident proposition that nothing can come out of nothing, whatever exists must have a cause for its existence. It is also certain that the cause must be as great as the effect, there must be at least as much reality in the cause as in the effect. Where do we get the idea of God? I myself can't be the cause of the idea of God, far my doubt shows that I am a finite and imperfect being. This idea can only be implanted in us by a Being that possesses in His own nature, the complete fullness of every perfection. Does the idea of a perfect and infinite being not have for its cause an actually existing being who is perfect and infinite? Therefore God as the most perfect being and infinite being exists. In this connection Descartes referred to the objection that the notion of the Infinite being is a negative idea that is acquired by means of mere abstraction and negation of the finite, as darkness is the negation of light. According to Descartes, the infinite has more reality than the finite and we get the notion of the finite after we get the notion of the Infinite. We cannot be conscious of our finitude unless we already possess the idea of the infinite in our minds.

(2) In the **second causal argument** or proof for the existence of God, Descartes, instead of searching for the cause of the idea of infinite and perfect being, searches for the cause of himself who has such an idea. Descartes argues that he himself cannot be the cause of his own existence. For if he had been the cause of his own existence, he could have created himself with all the perfections that is possible for him to think. But in spite of the fact that he possesses an idea of perfection in his mind, he is imperfect himself which would not have been the case if he were his own cause. Our parents even cannot be regarded as the cause of our existence for they are also not able to preserve us. Descartes comes to the conclusion that we and all other finite things owe their existence to God who is Himself existent or causa sui (self-caused). So from my existence, the existence of God is proved.

Several **objections** have been raised against this. The Empiricists think the idea of the infinite to be a negative idea. According to them we get the idea of infinite by denying the finite. So we cannot prove the existence of God from a negative idea. Descartes, however, claims that the idea of infinite is a positive idea, in which background we understand the finite to be finite. As Wright observes "We should not know that anything is finite unless in some sense we already knew the finite."

Secondly, it is said against Descartes that he has taken the causal law as a self-evident truth. In fact, the law is applicable with reference to empirical events. It is not applicable beyond this world or to God.

The **third proof** for the existence of God, as given by Descartes, is a priori proof for the existence of God. Here Descartes proves the existence of God from the very idea of God by simply analysing its content. It follows from the very notion of God as a most perfect being that He exists. As Descartes himself puts it: "It is not within my power to think of God without existence (that is, of a supremely perfect being devoid of a supreme perfection) though it is in my power to imagine a horse either with or without wings."

It follows from the very notion of God as a perfect being that He exists. The idea of the most perfect Being not only possesses like all other ideas the possibility of existence, i.e. the contingent existence, the most perfect being necessarily exists, for if it does not exist, in reality, and is merely an idea, then we can easily conceive of another being who is not only an idea but also existent. The idea of the most perfect being who exists is more perfect than the idea of the most perfect being who does not exist. But more perfect than most perfect is a contradiction in terms. Therefore the most perfect being exists. "When I examine the idea of a perfect being, I find that the existence of such a Being is implied in the idea in the same way as the equality of the three angles to two right angles is implied in the idea of a triangle—" "I cannot conceive anything but God Himself to whose essence existence pertains."

This is the famous **ontological argument** for the existence of God. A very similar argument was put forward by St. Anselm and St. Augustine in the **Middle Ages**.

VIII. Objections Against Descartes Proofs for the Existence of God

In criticism of Descartes' proofs for the existence of God we may say that Descartes has not put forward sufficient justification for the occurrence of the idea of God in our minds. He seems to take it as one item among others and as occurring somehow within our mind. He would have greatly strengthened his position if he had shown that the idea of God is one which we cannot dispense with and of which we must be conscious if we are to be conscious of our own finitude and imperfections. We must possess within our mind a standard, an idea of infinite and all-perfect being in comparison with whom we know ourselves to be finite and imperfect. Of course Descartes had all these things implicitly in his mind when he pronounced the idea of the Infinite to be a positive idea. The idea of the Infinite and necessary being does not arise by abstraction and negation of what is finite and contingent being. "The idea of the infinite is prior to that of the finite." But Descartes should have shown more explicitly that the idea of the infinite being is bound up with our finite consciousness in such a manner that-in being conscious of ourselves, we are conscious at the same time of existence of an infinite all-perfect being. His Cogito, ergo sum assures him of his own consciousness but he should have gone further and shown that the consciousness of which we are certain is not an individual isolated consciousness of which we are certain but one that is vitally and essentially bound up with an universal consciousness which is finite and all-perfect.

Against the causal arguments of Descartes it has been said that he assumes the law of causation without criticism and then applies it to God. Kant afterwards says in criticism that the principle of causation is a category of the understanding and, as such, it cannot be applied beyond the range of experience, i.e., to God. If we assume that every event must have a cause and from that prove the existence of God from the existence of ourselves as effect, we shall have to ask further question: What is the cause of God?"—a question which cannot be answered. A philosopher should not assume any principle dogmatically but must at first examine it critically and determine how far it is applicable.

Descartes' Ontological proof has been criticised by some of his contemporaries and also by Kant in later days. In his Ontological proof Descartes has simply analysed the idea of God and has deduced his existence from idea. Descartes has passed from idea to existence, from thought to reality, directly but, according to Kant, **from the idea of God we may only get the idea of existence**. To prove real existence we must have actual experience. Existence, Kant thinks, is not contained in the conception of anything. We can say a thing exists only when we meet with it in experience. Or are able to show that it can be experienced. Kant says that if reality would have been deduced from thought then the mere thinking of hundred dollars would have brought the dollars into existence. But such is not the case. Similarly, the idea of God can never lead us to his real existence. Again, from the idea of a triangle there certainty follows the equality of its angles to two right angles. But if the idea of triangle be dispensed with, the equality of its angles to two right angles is also dispensed with. In much the same way we can dispense with the idea of God as also his existence.

Descartes admits that we cannot pass from idea to existence. Idea of existence, and actual existence are different. Idea of God as the most perfect being may have idea of existence but we should remember that the idea of the most perfect being is not like any other idea. It is a necessary idea so that it proves its actual existence as soon as we possess the idea. This idea is not like any other contingent idea, like the dollars in my pocket, or the triangle, or a most perfect island. Idea of God is an exceptional idea as it is a necessary idea. Existence follows necessarily from the Idea of God as the most perfect Being.

Descartes' causal argument as well as Ontological argument has also been criticised as involving the fallacy of arguing in a circle. His first existential proposition beyond all doubt was I think therefore **I am**. At this stage he denied the existence of everything, even God. But from his consciousness as an existent being, and from the innate ideas in his mind, Descartes later proved the existence of God. The knowledge of my existence is prior to the knowledge of God's existence. Now, after proving God's existence, Descartes claims that.

It should have been shown by Descartes that it would not be so easy to dispense with the idea of God as it is a necessary idea and is intimately bound up with our finite consciousness. It is one thing to suppose a triangle to be non-existent, but it is quite another thing to suppose God to be non-existent. To apply the same argument to the idea of God and to the idea of triangle is a mistake.

On the whole, the argument of Descartes for the existence of God are weak in their original form. It should be shown that the idea of God is an idea which no rational thinker can avoid. Its necessary implication is that it cannot but be expected as true. The idea of God is necessary for the interpretation of all our actual experience:

Knowledge is not possible unless the world we know and the mind with which we know it, both proceed from the same source. Hence, if knowledge is not to fall in a chaos, the idea of God is necessary to explain it.

It was a necessity with Descartes to prove the existence of God in order to escape from Solipsism. To establish the existence of the external world, Descartes not only depends upon (1) existence of God, but also on the (2) veracity and truthfulness of God. In his initial sweeping doubt, Descartes had doubted away the existence of bodies outside us on the ground that though our sensations seem to refer to bodies outside as their causes, we cannot prove the existence of bodies from these experiences as they often deceive us. But now the existence of God as a perfect being demonstrated, the passage from these experiences to the external word becomes easy. We know whatever exists must have a cause and these experiences also must have their causes. There are two possibilities: either God has produced these experiences in us, with their corresponding references to bodies outside, whereas there are actually no bodies corresponding to them **or** these experiences have as their causes real things existing outside us. If the former hypothesis be true then God is a deceiver for He produces in our minds, with the purpose of deceiving, the ideas of things existing outside us, when there are no actual things really existing.

But this hypothesis must be discarded. God has been proved to be a most perfect Being and a perfect being must be veracious. God as a perfect being can never deceive his creatures. Therefore the other alternative viz., that there are real bodies external to us—must be accepted as true. We possess in our minds the clear and distinct idea that there are bodies outside of us and this idea must be true, for God has imposed this idea in our mind and God is a veracious being.

IX. Theory of Truth and Error

But if we are never deceived how is it that we ever commit error at all? Here Descartes gives his **theory** of **truth and error**. According to him error arises wherever there is discord between the cognition and faculty of election i.e., between understanding and will. So long as mind is passive there is no error. But by means of our power of free choice we either affirm or deny some or all of the ideas that we receive through sense perception. But sometimes it so happens that our will, instead of following the dictates of our understanding, chooses the false instead of the true; that is, passes judgment on something of which we have not sufficiently clear and distinct idea. Here will falls into error. God being veracious, whatever the human mind clearly and distinctly perceives is true. Mind in its passive attitude can never commit any error. **The veracity of God therefore is another criterion of truth for Descartes.**

Descartes himself said earlier "I call that **clear** which is present and apparent to an attentive mind. But the **distinct** is that which is so precise and different from all other objects that it contains within itself nothing but what is clear." (Principle of Philosophy). "This criterion of truth", says Copleston, "was doubtless suggested to Descartes by mathematics." Thus whatever is clearly and distinctly perceived by our understanding is true. Clearness and distinctness of an idea amounts to its truth—these are identical. So it can be said that Descartes' criterion of truth is self-evident.

X. Descartes, Proving the Reality of the External World

On the basis of **this criterion of truth** viz, clearness and distinctness of ideas, Descartes proves his own existence only, to the exclusion of everything else—the other minds, the external world, even God has not been proved. Descartes proves the existence of God mainly by ontological argument. The idea of God is such that His existence follows necessarily from His idea. Now he has to prove the reality of the external world. Here he shifts from his original criterion of clearness and distinctness of ideas to the veracity of God. God being the most perfect Being, cannot be a deceiver. So, the external world which corresponds to our ideas of the external world, and which are produced by God in our minds as clear and distinct ideas, may now be taken as true. Here his criterion of Truth is the veracity of God. He declares now that the clearness and distinctness of ideas of human mind must be regarded as true because God is a veracious being—he has imposed these ideas in our minds. Thus here his criterion of truth is not clearness and distinctness of ideas but truthfulness of God. So Descartes' argument is circular. He bases the existence of God on clearness and distinctness of our ideas (Innate idea of God) and again the truth of clear and distinct ideas on the veracity of God.

Erdmann has given a very good defence against this charge of circularity of reasoning. He points out that there is no circularity in Descartes' reasoning, for, from the point of view of existence God comes first and produce the clear and distinct ideas in our minds. In the order of knowledge however, the clear and distinct ideas come first and we know God through such ideas. As Prof. Falkenberg observes "In the order of existence God is first, creates the reason together with its criterion; in the order of knowledge the criterion precedes and God's existence follows from it. The criterion of certitude is the "ratio cognoscendi" of God's existence and God is the "ratio essendi" of criterion of certitude.

The most popular **objection raised against Descartes' criterion of truth** is that his criterion gives us only "subjective" truth. Clearness and distinctness of ideas is a subjective criterion as it varies from individual to individual. What is clear and distinct to one may not be such to another person. The same thing may seem clear and distinct to one, and not clear and distinct to another. Thus the very objectivity of the criterion is lost. It is thus not possible to arrive at universal truths through Descartes' criterion.

This objection also may be refuted by saying that Descartes has meant by the words "clear and distinct" is understanding's direct contact with object, in which 'will' has not yet interfered. Our will is responsible for our errors, said Descartes, because it actively chooses from the sense-manifold. The natural light, which God has given to human understanding, illuminates any idea clearly and distinctly without the intervention of will (our likes and dislikes)—it is universally true.

Again, some philosophers raise the objection that Descartes' criterion of Truth (clearness and distinctness) proves adequately the existence of the self only, but it is not so evidently applicable to other cases like the 'existence of God', 'Every event must have a cause' etc. These require rational arguments.

This objection cannot be easily met. As Descartes himself puts it, "there is some difficulty in ascertaining which are those (things) that we distinctly perceive".

XI. Theory of Substance

The existence of bodies external to us has been proved. Bodies exist independently of our thinking and do not need our existence in order to exist. Such an independent thing is called a substance. **According to Descartes, a substance is that which requires for its existence, the existence of nothing else**. In this highest sense only God is Substance. God as the Infinite substance has the ground of His existence in Himself and is the Absolute Substance. But besides God there are two relative substances viz., mind and matter. Mind and Matter are substances in the less restricted sense of the term. They depend for their existence only upon God but they are independent and different from each other. The attribute or **essential property of matter is extension and that of mind is thought**. One is the negation of the other. This is the Dualism of Descartes. This theory of two kinds of primary substances is responsible for many of Descartes' problems and had a lasting influence in the history of subsequent philosophy.

Modes are the accidental qualities of a substance, which are known as **secondary qualities**. These modes or secondary qualities are not essential for the substances, because these modes are sometimes present in a substance and sometimes not. The secondary quality of matter is position, shape and motion etc. The secondary qualities of mind substance are willing, feeling etc. **The primary qualities** on the essential properties of substances do not change, only the secondary qualities change. God being immutable and unchangeable has no modes.

Thus there are three substances in Descartes' philosophy—(1) God, (2) Matter, and (3) Mind. God is the **absolute substance** because He alone is self-dependent, depends on nothing for His existence, but mind and matter are **Relative substances**, depending for their existence on God.

In criticism against Descartes' doctrine of substance, we can say that, according to his own definition of substance, there should be only one substance, viz., God.

Again, matter and mind, being opposed to each other by nature, the problem of mind-body relation arises from Descartes' dualism of substances.

There arises another dualism regarding God and His relation to the world. God is the creator of the world but the world of things and beings remain outside God. Thus there is one God on the one hand, and the world on the other hand. God, remaining outside the world makes the world limited, the world also remaining outside God. Such a God cannot be treated as an all-perfect being.

Matter is the antithesis of mind and has for its essential attribute extension. Descartes divides the properties of matter into two kinds viz., primary and secondary. Extension is the primary quality of matter. It is the very essence of matter, that without which matter cannot be conceived. Secondary qualities are variable and do not exist in the things in themselves, e.g., colour, taste, smell etc. Descartes makes no distinction between spaciality and materiality. Hence he does not believe in empty space. As extension is not a substance by itself but is only a property of matter, it cannot exist by itself. Bodies have two states of motion and rest. But matter conceived as mere extension is passive and cannot move by itself. Descartes takes recourse to God as the first cause of motion in the world. The quantity of motion in the world is constant as God's nature is immutable and God is the primary cause of all motions.

Descartes thinks that everything in this world, up to the human body, can be explained by means of mechanical principles. We are too imperfect and too ignorant to aspire for knowledge of God's motive in creating the world. According to Descartes the world requires God's constant intervention to keep it going. This is his **theory** of **perpetual creation**.

Living things are, for him, nothing more than complex machines. God being perfect has been able to construct machines infinitely more perfect than man. This is the only difference between a living body and a man-made clock. The human body is also a machine and in this respect has no higher status than the animal.

XII. Problem of Mind-Body Relation

Descartes solves the **problem of mind-body relation** in the following way: According to him, mind and matter are absolutely opposed substances. He has also said that human body is simply a machine, material out and out. Now the question arises—how these two opposed substances are brought together to explain the intimate correspondence between mind and body in the case of human beings? According to Descartes, the relation between mind and body is only a mechanical one. Human body is simply a machine and, within this machine, in the Pineal Gland of the brain, mind is situated. From this position mind influences body. This is known as the **Interactionism Theory of Mind-Body Relation**.

But this is no explanation. How can mind which is spiritual and non-extended have a position and how can it influence that which is absolutely opposed to it? This has not been made clear in Descartes' theory. Descartes' immediate followers, the **Occasionalists**, try to solve this problem by saying that mind and body cannot be brought together; but on the occasion of certain movements in the body certain sensations are produced in the mind not directly but through the intervention of God. Whatever that may be, the problem arises for Descartes only because of his fundamental dualism of mind and matter and all subsequent philosophers try to solve this problem each in his own way.

There are many drawbacks in Descartes' theories of self, God, world, Mind-Body relation etc. But he gave us a systematic and rational philosophy on most of the philosophical problems. We may conclude with F. Copleston by saying that 'In his History of Philosophy Hegel salutes Descartes as the real originator of modern philosophy, whose chief merit is to have started from "thought" without presuppositions.'

Benedict Spinoza

(1634-1677)

4

CHAPTER

I. His Life and Works

Spinoza was born a Jew in 1634 in Holland. His ancestors lived in Spain. But in fear of torture they shifted to Holland. He was educated in Jewish learning but was not at all orthodox. He studied Mathematics thoroughly, liked Geometry and Natural Sciences, was influenced by Descartes views on God, soul etc. He endeavoured throughout his life to show that the scriptures can be interpreted in the light of Reason, and may be interpreted so as to be compatible with a liberal theology. His original thinking clashed with the views of both the Jews and the Christians. The priests were so angry with him that they labelled him as an atheist. He refused an offer in the University of Hydelberg as it was offered with a view to curtail his independent thinking. Spinoza possessed some rare qualities. The Jewish rabbi (The Synagogue) excommunicated him, and he was left alone. His relatives and friends avoided his company. Spinoza was not at all moved by this situation. He settled in Hague and led a quiet and simple life. Money, Fame and Power was not his aim. He aimed at moulding his life-style in the light of Truth. He not only believed in his own doctrine but practised them throughout his life. He made his living by polishing glasses. It is an irony of fate that Spinoza, with whom God was the first and last word of his life and philosophy—was treated as an atheist by his contemporaries. At the early age of forty-three he died of Pthisis.

His chief work was the 'Ethics' which was published posthumously. Spinoza's Philosophy has been interpreted in many ways by various thinkers. It has been called **Pantheism** by one, again non-theistic **Naturalism** by others, **Idealism** as well as

Materialism, Spiritualism, as well as Naturalism. Some interpret Spinoza as **atheiet**, others again, as a **God-intoxicated man**. All these judgments represent facts in Spinoza himself. From the standpoint of orthodox theology, there is no doubt that Spinoza is irreligious, for he denounces the personal God of the Christian religion, the Government of the world according to purpose and freedom of the will. It is often difficult to distinguish his theory from thoroughgoing naturalism which identifies God with the necessary laws of the physical universe. But Spinoza himself regards the ordinary conception of God as false and thinks that he is indicating the only worthy idea of religion. God is the beginning and end of his philosophy and hence his title "God-intoxicated man".

II. Spinoza's Method

Like Descartes, Spinoza is a Rationalist. Self-evidence is for him the test of truth. He accepts the Mathematical method introduced by Descartes and uses it more vigorously. Spinoza wanted to start from some definite premises and to build up his own philosophy by irrefutable arguments, so that his philosophy would attain the certainty of a book of **Euclid**. But though Descartes starts with the irrefutable 'Cogito, ergo sum", he fails to deduce the whole philosophy from the same. What Spinoza aims at is a system of knowledge in which everything should necessarily follow from self-evident axioms and definitions. Propositions following from them will stretch logical necessity. In Geometry everything follows with strict logical necessity from the fundamental conception of Space. In philosophy Spinoza begins with the conception of God, the ultimate substance, as if it were a mathematical concept from which everything else could be deduced. God is the logical ground of the world, not its cause in the ordinary sense of the term. God does not create the world with a purpose in view, but the world follows logically from His nature, just as the equality of its angles to two right angles follows from the nature of a triangle.

But from the very nature of it a purely **Geometrical** method is inadequate to the treatment of **philosophical** truths. Geometry starts with some axioms or postulates or definitions, on the basis of which newer and newer truths are deduced. The conclusions are as certain as the original self-evident axioms. Spinoza applied this Geometrical method very cautiously and carefully in his most famous book "Ethics". He begins with the concept of substance and deduces from substance the entire world of finite things and beings.

Let us see why this Geometrical method is not adequate for philosophy:

(1) Firstly, Geometry starts with certain assumptions which it does not critically examine. Philosophy, however, admits of no unexamined presupposition.

(2) Secondly, Spinoza supposes that the particular figures of Geometry viz., triangle, square etc. logically follow from the idea of space. But, as a matter of fact, though these figures presuppose space, there is no reason in the idea of space as to why these figures should exist. The fundamental conception of Geometry is **Sterile** in the sense that it has not the principle of its own self-development within itself. This defect is inherent in Spinoza's philosophy. He cannot point out the reason why the world of finite objects should necessarily follow from the nature of the ultimate substance.

(3) Thirdly, the mathematical method can never be applied successfully in philosophy because it is an **abstract method.** Geometry means abstraction of the quantitative aspect of things from all its other aspects. Life, however, is qualitative as well as quantitative. The abstract categories of mathematics, therefore, cannot be applied to the concrete sphere of philosophy.

(4) Again, deductive method of geometry or mathematics does not allow new knowledge. It is necessary and certain but it does not increase our knowledge. So philosophy cannot accept geometrical or mathematical method as its own method.

(5) If the existence of world is deduced from the idea of God as substance, then the world will not be temporal. It will be something beyond time. Spinoza himself says that the world is not created by God at a particular time, it follows necessarily from God as substance. The world is eternal, beyond time.

(6) Sixthly, if everything follows from God as substance, with Geometrical necessity, then there is no freedom of will.

(7) Seventhly, a true philosophy could be presented without the use of geometrical adornments and forms. Conversely, a false philosophy could be presented in a geometrical dress—observes F. Copleston.

III. Spinoza's Theory of Substance

The starting point of Spinoza's philosophy is the idea of substance. "By substance I mean that which is in itself and **is conceived through itself** i.e., that the conception of which does not need the conception of any other thing in order to its formation". This substance Spinoza identifies with God; whom he defines as "a being absolutely infinite i.e., a substance which consists of infinite number of attributes of which each expresses an eternal and infinite essence".

Besides God, no substance can be or be conceived, "whatever is, is in God, and without God nothing can be or be conceived".

From this it follows that God must be "causes sui", or his own cause. If he were not so, he would be produced by something else and, therefore, would not be substance in the strict sense of the term.

Secondly, substance must be **infinite**, for, if it were not so it would be limited by and dependent on something else, and, therefore, would not be substance at all. For the same reason, there can be only one substance.

It follows further that God, or the substance, acts solely by the laws of His own nature and is not controlled by anyone else. God is the sole free cause, free in the sense that He does nothing except that towards which His own nature impels Him. Spinoza's conception **of freedom** thus excludes constraint on the one hand, and caprice on the other. God is free but He cannot act arbitrarily as all His actions must follow logically from His own nature.

It follows further that God cannot act with a purpose in view. To suppose that God acts with an end in view is to make God aim at something beyond Him. But there is nothing beyond Him. Besides, God has no deficiency in His nature which he may want to get rid of and hence we cannot ascribe final cause to God. According to Spinoza, God creates the world with a purpose in view no more than the triangle voluntarily makes its three angles equal to two right angles (consequence). God is the ground, the world is the consequence, just as triangle is the ground and its angles being equal to two right angles—is its consequence.

Thus the God of Spinoza is not the God of ordinary theism. God is not the external transcendent cause of the world, acting on it from without (Deism), but is in the world, as the immanent principle of the universe. God is in the world and the world is in God. He is the source of everything that is (Pantheism). God is the permanent substratum or essence of everything. As the active principle or the source of all reality, Spinoza calls God the **Natura Naturus**. Again, as the Plurality of objects, God is called by Spinoza, the **Natura Naturata**. This phrase needs some explanation. If, as the definition of substance or God suggests, the world cannot exist over and above God. Substance is infinite and it is one. So Spinoza concludes that the world as a whole is God. The finite selves and finite material objects of this world are modes of the substance. These modes or modifications of substance as a whole is called by Spinoza as "**Natura Naturata**; and the substance as infinite and one, is **Natura Naturars**." The difference between the two is not real, it is only a difference of outlook. So what is God or Substance is the same as what is this world. As Copleston puts it "it is not empirical Nature which is identified with God, but rather Nature in a peculiar sense, as the infinite substance, which lies behind the transitory modes."

Such a theory of God as inherent in everything is popularly known as Pantheism. But Spinoza's Pantheism does not take God as qualified by any human quality, or moral character. This substance is a mathematical or mechanical system. Spinoza gives the equation—**Substance = God = Nature**. The impersonal ground of this world is the Substance. This substance Spinoza identifies with God. His God is not the personal God of religion, who creates this world, but He is the sum total of all realifies. So Spinoza identifies these two with Nature, i.e., the sum-total of all finite things and beings. This new conception of God as impersonal, the principle of Unity in Nature, went against Christianity and Spinoza was called an atheist.

According to Spinoza we cannot ascribe any human characteristics to God, for all determinations (quality) are negations (limitations)—**"Determinatio negatio est"**. For Spinoza a determination takes that which distinguishes one thing from another, hence, what it is not i.e., expresses a limitation of it. If we say 'the flower is red', it at once affirms that the flower is not not-red, (white or yellow etc.), and thus limits it. So the Substance has no determinations, (Nirguna). God who is free from every negation and limitation is to be conceived as absolutely indeterminate.

If substance be indeterminate and abstract, and if this abstract unity be the only reality then it follows that the differences existing apparently in this world are unreal. Such view of substance has often been compared to a **'lion's den'**—to which many footsteps can be traced but from which no footsteps can be seen as coming out. As J. Caind says, "Spinoza's Substance is reached not be reconciliation of opposed but related elements in a higher unity, but simply abstracting from the difference of these elements. It not only contains in it no principle of self-determination, but it is itself the negation of all determination." Such a view of Substance cannot explain the world. But Spinoza's conception of substance is somewhat ambiguous. Sometimes he takes substance in a pantheistic manner as the concrete unity of all things. According to this view God is the sum-total of all realities.

IV. Spinoza's Doctrine of Attributes and Modes

To explain the variety of existence Spinoza formulates the **doctrine of Attributes and Modes.** Spinoza defines attributes as that "which the intellect perceives as constituting the essence of substance".

God or Substance consists of infinite number of "attributes of which each expresses an eternal and infinite essence". Of these infinite number of attributes, only two—thought and extension—can be known by human intelligence. In one sense each of the attributes of God is infinite. For it completely represents the nature of God from one particular point of view. Thought is infinite in its own sphere, but it is not absolutely infinite, for it is limited by extension and other attributes. God is absolutely infinite: the attributes only in their kind. By his doctrine of attributes Spinoza tries to solve the **problem** of **the relation of mind and matter** which Descartes had failed to solve. Thought and extension are not as with Descartes two distinct and opposed substances but two attributes of one and the same substance—two points of view from which the same substance may be apprehended. There is no connection left, and no need for any. The attributes of substance are parallel to each other. Corresponding to every mode of thought, there is a mode of extension. None is superior to the other. Spinoza is opposed both to Spiritualism and Materialism, one of which tries to explain matter in terms of mind and the other—mind in terms of matter.

V. Spinoza's Theory of Mind-Body Relation

One of the principal traditional theories on the relation between mind and body is **Parallelism**. According to Spinoza, mental processes and physical processes run parallel to each other. The theory is also known as Psycho-Physical Parallelism.

Spinoza arrived at his Parallelism by criticising Descartes' theory of Interactionism. According to Descartes' Substance is that which exists by itself. There are three substances for Descartes: God is the Absolute substance, mind and matter are two relative substances. These depend on God for their existence. The essential character of mind-substance is consciousness, and the essential character of matter substance is extension, so that these two substances are opposed to each other in nature. What is consciousness is not extension and what is extension is not consciousness.

But in human body we find these substances acting causally on each other. Mental events like 'anger' cause physical event like 'striking' upon the object. Descartes explained the fact as Interactionism. According to him, mind is situated in a part of the body, the pineal gland in our brain, and, from there, it influences the body.

Spinoza asks here: How can mind, which is essentially consciousness, occupy space and **sit** in the Pineal Gland of human brain which is part of the physical body? How can two independent substances **interact** causally? Spinoza rejects Descartes' theory and puts forward his Parallelism.

According to Spinoza, just as two parallel lines never meet, similarly mind and body, mental states and physical states run parallel to each other and never meet together to influence each other. Moreover, mind and matter are not two independent substances. Consciousness and extension are two attributes of one substance God; two points of view from which the same substance may be apprehended. "It is as if the two kinds of events occurred along two parallel tracks without even touching one another."—says Hospers. For every mental event, there is a corresponding physical event in our brain.

Spinoza says that one mental event can cause another mental event, and one physical event can cause another physical event, but no mental event can produce any change in physical event. They only run parallel. Attributes of Substance are not basically different. They are just different points of view from which the 'one' and the 'same' Substance is apprehended.

Suppose I see a beautiful red rose and stretch my hand to pluck it. Here the stretching of my hand is not a mental event at all, but a series of brain-events which, in turn, stimulate nerves muscles etc. I stretch my hand. The entire series of causes and effects can be traced in the physical realm. But, along with these physical events, events in consciousness also occur, mental events like volition, pleasure etc. also occur simultaneously. But they are not caused by those physical events. "Parallelism here includes the mental events, since of course parallelism does not deny that they occur. It is only their acting as causes and effects that parallelism denies."—says J. Hospers.

In fact, Interactionism emphasises upon causal connection between mind and body. Parallelism says: mind and body do not depend on each other causally. The dispute thus seems to be verbal (linguistic)—as to the meaning of the word "causal".—says Hospers

As Copleston observes: "Spinoza's doctrine about the relation between mind and body must be true if his general doctrine of substance and its attributes is true but the word 'if' is here of some importance." Later philosophers find many faults with his theory of Substance, attributes and their relation, his geomentrical method as applied to philosophy, his monism etc. His parallelism also is not accepted by many philosophers. In our experience we often see that every physical object or event is not accompanied by a corresponding mental state, e.g. we do not have any mental state running parallel to our digestion or blood-circulation.

We observe that sometimes even our body influences our mind. e.g. a sudden pain in my stomach makes me anxious. Again, if we accept Spinoza's psycho-physical parallelism, then wherever there is a physical object or event, there must be a mental event corresponding to it, which is not the case, e.g. the stars, the mountains, the rivers and seas, have no consciousness.

So Spinoza's theory of mind-body relation is not satisfactory, it fails to answer the question: **Why** mind and body run always parallel to each other without causally influencing each other?

VI. Relation between Substance and Attributes

There is a controversy as to what according to Spinoza is the exact **relation between Substance and Attributes**; whether the attributes are merely what our understanding ascribes to the substance or do they possess any reality apart from the knowing subject? Does Spinoza mean that the attributes really constitute the essence of substance, or does he mean that the substance is the abstract and indeterminate unity and attributes are ascribed to it by the human intellect?

According to **Kuno Fischer** and others, attributes belong to the essence of substance. The attributes are more than mere modes of representation. They are real properties which substance possesses even apart from an observer. God or Substance is the concrete unity of all things, hence the sum total of all attributes.

But this view cannot be reconciled with the doctrine of Spinoza viz., that Substance is the indeterminate absolute of which all determinations are negations. **"Determinatio negation est"**. There is nothing in the nature of substance which can logically justify these attributes. Spinoza gives no reasons why the attributes should belong to the substance.

Though Spinoza gives no reason, the motive which led him to ascribe attributes to substance is not difficult to understand.

As Caird says, "Had Spinoza not refused to be led by his own logic, his system would have ended where it began. Philosophy along with other things comes to an end in a principle which reduces all thought and being to nothingness". Moreover, "it is impossible to think an affirmation which affirms nothing in particular or is a pure blaind affirmation devoid of all negations."

Hegel and Erdman, however, interpret Spinoza to mean that attributes do not and cannot belong to the nature of Substance which is indeterminate. But they are ascribed to the Substance by the human intellect. Substance itself is neither extended, nor cogitative but merely appears to the human understanding under these determinations; without which the latter (human understanding) would be unable to cognise it.

But this formal and strict interpretation of Spinoza's doctrine renders at once the solution of the problem of mind and matter, as given by Spinoza, absolutely meaningless. For if mind and matter do not really belong to the essence of substance, then there is no justification to assume that they are parallel throughout. This view also involves argument in a circle. Attributes are said not to belong to substance but merely ascribed to substance or imagined to exist in substance by the finite intellect. Which is only a mode of an attribute, i.e. thought.

But finite intellect is itself only a mode or modification of one of the attributes of substance. The attributes therefore exist only through that which is simply a modification of one of them. Finite intelligence is supposed to create that by which it is itself created. In fact, Hegel and Erdmann emphasise the first part of Spinoza's definition of attributes ("... that which the **intellect perceives** as constituting the essence of substance".) and give an idealistic interpretation of Spinoza's theory of the relation between the substance and the attributes. While Kuno Fishcher and others emphasise the last part the definition ("... as consistituting the **essence** of substance") giving thus a realistic interpretation of attributes. The qualified substance is the inner essence of the whole world. **Natura naturata have** been produced **by the Natura Naturans**. Such a qualified Monism is similar to Ramanuja's Visitadvaita Vedanta of Indian Philosophy.

Spinoza's doctrine of attributes is, thus, ambiguous and has given rise to much controversy. It is difficult to determine which of the above views Spinoza really held for passages from Spinoza may be quoted to support both the views.

Spinoza, however, found out a way by which it was possible for him to ascribe attributes to the substance without destroying its purely indeterminate nature viz., by distinguishing between what is **"absolutely infinite"** and what is "only **infinite in its own kind."** The attributes which Spinoza ascribed to the substance were not finite but infinite, not negative but positive and, hence, limited by neither the infinite substance nor by each other.

According to Spinoza all finite distinctions disappear in the infinite. The attributes, however, are not finite since no one of them is limited by the rest or anything within its own sphere. Each one of the different attributes expresses the same infinite reality and the whole of that reality.

But, as Caird has rightly pointed out "The objectivity of the attributes cannot be maintained by this device. The attributes, though said to be infinite each in its own kind, are not really different in kind. The content of each is just the same as that of any other and the difference is only a difference in our ways of looking at it . . . Spinoza's reconciliation of diversity of attributes with absolute self-identical unity of substance is simply that the diversity is a purely subjective one."

In Criticism of Spinoza's Doctrine of Attributes

(1) We can say that Spinoza supplies us with no reason why mind and matter should be attributes of God. They are merely assumed to belong to God.

(2) Again, Spinoza gives no reason as to the fact that, if there is an infinite number of attributes belonging to God, why human intellect knows only about two of them—mind and matter.

(3) And if it knows only two of them, how does it come to know that there are others and infinite number of attributes parallel to each other?

(4) Moreover, though Spinoza holds that mind and matter are parallel throughout, he is not always consistent with his own view. Mind perceives matter but matter cannot perceive mind. Towards the end of his philosophy Spinoza says that mind can become immortal by leading a spiritual life, but he does not show how matter can likewise become immortal.

(5) The attributes, even if legitimately deduced, leave us still in the region of the infinite and furnish us with no clue to the finite world. The attributes are pseudo-infinite in which there is nothing to point to anything beyond themselves.

VII. Spinoza's Doctrine of Modes and Thin Relation to Substance

Spinoza's doctrine of **modes and their relation to substance** is an attempt to explain the existence of the finite world and its relation to the infinite. Spinoza attempts to derive the many from the one and the changing from the eternal by his doctrine of modes.

By mode, says Spinoza, **"I mean the modification of the Substance** or that which exists in and is conceived through something other than itself." The modes are, therefore, the actual finite objects of the universe. They exist in the Substance and are conceived through the Substance. They have no independent reality of their own. The attributes Thought and Extension are infinite. They represent the intellectual and the material sphere of existence. But the modes of thought and extension represent the finite and particular minds and bodies of the world. Corresponding to every mode of thought, there is a mode of extension e.g., there is a particular body corresponding to every particular mind.

VIII. The Relation of Modes with Attributes

on of the modes to the attributes is left unexplained by Spinoza. If modes are finite and the attributes are infinite, how to explain their reference to one another? Spinoza makes a last attempt to solve the problem of the relation between infinite and the finite in his conception of **"Infinite modes"**. These are the immediate modifications of attributes. As an example of an infinite mode of extension Spinoza mentions "motion". Motion itself is infinite though particular causes of motion are finite. This affords a seeming connection between the infinite substance and the finite objects of the world. But even the infinite modes are infinite. So the origin of the finite world of particular remain as obscure as ever.

In connection with the origin and status of the system of finite modes Spinoza is faced with the same difficulty as he had in connection with the attributes. Spinoza sometimes says—

(a) that the modes follow from the nature of substance with as much necessity as particular properties follow from the nature of geometrical figures.

Modes seem to be the actual finite and temporal parts of the Substance which is itself infinite and eternal. But how can the Substance, which is immutable, be modified? Hence there has been another interpretation of Spinoza's theory of modes viz., (b) that Substance is not modified at all, but modes are mere appearances. The Natura Naturata iş nothing but imperfect conception of a finite intellect. If we take a view of all things under the form of eternity, we perceive that the particular modes are unreal and that the substance is the only reality.

What then are we? If the world of modes be a world of unreal appearances, then we ourselves are unreal. But how can the unreal finite intelligence have so much reality that it can imagine the unreal to be real?

In fact, Spinoza's theory of modes is founded on a presupposition that—the world of modes follows with geometrical necessity from God or substance. But this presupposition is only a baseless imagination. From an idea, what follows necessarily is also an idea, not the reality. The properties of a triangle follows necessarily from the idea of a triangle, but those are only ideas of properties, not real properties. So, logically, the world of finite things and beings (the Natura Naturata) does not follow from the infinite and One Substance or God. The eternal unchanging substance cannot explain this changing world of objects.

As Hegel puts it, "Spinozism . . . might have been termed **Acosmism.** *Since according to its teaching, it is not to the world, finite existence, the universe that

*Acosmism is a doctrine which denies the reality of the finite world of things and beings. The Advaita Vedanta conception of world as 'illusion' may be called Acosmism. Sankaracharya denied this world. He equated Substance with God, and God with Nature. His motive was practical, as we shall see in his Ethics.

reality and permanency are to be ascribed, but rather to God alone as the Substantial". He has denied the world of many. It is difficult to establish the reality of the finite world of many from the one all-embracing Substance. Spinoza thus sacrificed plurality at the altar of unity, many at the cost of one. Like a lion's den, footsteps can be seen to enter into it, but no footsteps can be seen to be coming out. Many is an illusion, only God is real, because God alone is self-existent. Spinoza's metaphysics is Pantheism—All is God and God is all.

But we may say that this equation God = World may be treated in two ways: If we take it as God = World then Spinoza is an acosmist, but if we take the equation as, World = God, then Spinoza is not at all world-denying. Rather it can be said that, according to Spinoza, the variety and plurality of this world is basically supported by 'one' unifying principle and that is God. World is not an appearance or a mirage, but is real and God is inherent in each and every object of this world of many. This is Pantheism and Spinoza is called a 'God-intoxicated man'.

Thus we see that individuality remains unexplained in Spinoza's Philosophy. By no possibility could Spinoza connect the world of finite modes of existence in time with the true and eternal (timeless he means) reality of God and consequently he leaves the finite world without explanation. Logically he should have denied the finite world altogether. Yet he could not boldly declare the same, for his metaphysics is nothing but preparation for his ethics. His motive is mainly practical and the whole purpose of his philosophy is to show how man, being a part of the phenomenal world, can escape its finitude and attain true freedom. This much is his metaphysics. Now begins his Ethics.

IX. Spinoza's Ethics

Spinoza's motive in writing philosophy was mainly practical. It is the practical end of attaining real happiness by escaping from the miseries of finite world that led Spinoza to ponder over metaphysical problems.

According to Spinoza the dissatisfaction of life is due to the fact that our affections are set not upon an object that is eternal and unchanging but upon transitory and imperfect things. If the objects of our love were perfect and unchangeable, our passions would have been satisfied. But because we love that which has no consistency and true reality, we are in a continual turmoil of emotions and never know what peace is. If we **view all things "under the form of eternity**" we are no longer unduly influenced by them. Here Spinoza brings in the conception of **degrees of knowledge**. There are, according to him, three grades of knowledge. The **lowest** stage of knowledge is the vague experience called **opinion** or imagination. Here intelligence is governed by accidental and subjective associations and regards the world as made up of finite and independent objects. The **second** grade of knowledge is scientific knowledge—this is the next higher stage of reason where, though the finite objects are still regarded as real, their interconnections and laws are understood. We do not regard particular things as unrelated and isolated at this stage of knowledge, but suppose the world to be governed by universal laws and causal sequences. But the mind can know all things under the form of eternity only when it reaches the **highest stage** of knowledge, which Spinoza calls **intuition**. At this stage of knowledge, we find all the diversities integrated into one system. We form an adequate idea of God only at this stage.

According to Spinoza, every individual has got a "conatus"—a tendency to struggle for one's own existence. The essence of life is self-preservation or self-assertion. When this self-assertive activity depends only on ourselves we have what Spinoza calls an **"action"**. When it depends, in part, upon what lies beyond ourselves, it is called **"passion"**. In ordinary life we are under the sway of passions, we ascribe more reality to finite objects than they deserve. We are too much affected by temporary events—hence our restlessness, hopes, fears and disappointments. When the mind understands all things as necessarily following from the nature of God, it is no longer unduly influenced by them. So we should endeavour to attain the highest stage of knowledge where we would be able to view all things under the form of eternity. At this stage we are free and active in the truest sense of the term, for, we are never fully active except when we think truly and see things as they are in God. Though at first sight there seems hardly any room for freedom, in a system where everything follows necessarily from the nature of God, man is really free only at this stage of knowledge. For **freedom,** according to Spinoza, consists not in indeterminism but in self-determinism. While **bondage** is subjection to causation, freedom is self-activity. When a man understands all things under the form of eternity, he identifies his own nature with the nature of substance. So all his actions follows from his own nature. A man can attain freedom 'only by changing the idea of separate freedom'. Freedom is thus a life of reason as distinguished from bondage which is a life of opinion and passions. Liberation from bondage lies in man's realisation that whatever happens, happens with absolute necessity, from the very nature of Substance, and nothing else would have been possible.

Spinoza's doctrine of **immortality** of the human soul is the same as his doctrine of freedom. The actual existence of human being as a finite object is transitory but the essence is eternal. When a man attains the highest stage of knowledge, the illusion of time vanishes from the mind and the mind realises itself to be immortal, not as an isolated finite object but as an aspect of substance. This is perceiving everything under the form of eternity—"Sub specie Eternitatis." Time, for Spinoza, is real from the empirical point of view, so that the finite objects of the world live and act in time. But, for God, there is no time but only eternity.

Spinoza sums up all the characteristics of a perfect life by calling it an "intellectual love of God". This involves not the extinction of the whole of our emotional life but only of those emotions which tend to decrease our perfection. Our love should be detached from the finite and transitory objects of the world and should be attached to God. Spinoza does not advocate sacrifice or repentance, for, being painful, these processes are imperfect. **Virtue is pure bliss or blessedness. Happiness is not the reward of virtue, but identical with virtue itself**. "Whatever we understand by the third form of knowledge, we take delight in and our delight is accompanied by the idea of God as cause." This reminds us of the Upanishadic concept of "Sat-chit-anandam" of Vedanta of Indian Philosophy.

This intellectual love is the very love with which God loves Himself. For, man is a mode of God and in so far as God loves Himself He also loves men, because they are a part of Him. That indeterminate absolute substance of Spinoza's metaphysics becomes God who possesses freedom and intelligence and who loves the finite beings with an infinite and intellectual love.

The blessed life of Spinoza consists of perfect knowledge which is the same as perfect freedom and perfect bliss. Sin is identical with error, there is no such thing as deliberate vicious action. It seems, however, difficult to reconcile such a view with the experiences of actual life. Moreover, it is very difficult to understand how error could ever arise. How can the individual, who is in reality nothing apart from God, ever have the opportunity to think inadequate ideas from which our passions and our bondage arise?

If we accept Spinoza's eithics we should say that each and every event in this world is good, as these are produced with logical necessity from the nature of God or Substance. The critic like B. Russell will say here: "suppose you are a Jew, and your family has been massacred, . . . suppose your husband, for some imaginary crime has been sent to forced labour in the Arctic, and has died of cruelty and starvation. Ought you in these circumstances, to preserve a philosophic calm?"

Such an ethical calmness, as Spinoza advocates, is not supported by our moral sense. We believe, what is evil from our imperfect standpoint, is evil from the 'sub specie Aternitatis' (from the point of view of eternity) also.

Again, Spinoza says that all men necessarily strive after continuance of existence. This self-preservation is identical with virtue and knowledge. Why do then so few reach the goal? Whence do the powerless defective and ignorant natures come? If God is all and all is God and if the individual has no freedom of will, how can there be any imperfection in the universe? Spinoza explains this difficulty by saying that evil or imperfection expresses nothing positive or actual. Values are not actual properties of things but they are agreeable and disagreeable effects on us. Spinoza's ethics thus leaves hardly any room for the distinction between good and evil.

Spinoza's doctrine of freedom and immortality are inconsistent with his theory of parallelism. Though Spinoza says again and again that mind and matter are parallel throughout, he gives greater importance to mind than to matter. Mind can know matter but matter cannot know mind. Mind can gradually become more and more perfect and thus control the emotions and the body, but the body cannot do so. When mind becomes perfect it is free or its actions follow from its own nature. But no such provision is made for body. Finally, mind, in so far as it transcends itself to be an aspect of Substance, becomes immortal. But Spinoza does not show how the body can become immortal.

5

CHAPTER

G. W. Leibniz
(1646-1716)

I. His Life and Works

Leibniz was born at Leipzig in Germany in 1646, where his father was a professor of moral philosophy. He studied German language, Latin and Greek, and became acquainted with the writings of different philosophers and scientists like Herodotus, Plato, Aristotle and others. At the age of 15, he entered the Leipzig University to learn law, philosophy and mathematics. He learnt the philosophies of Bacon, Hobbes and Descartes. In 1666, he was offered Doctorate from Altdorf University and was also offered a professorship there. But he refused.

He went to Paris and England and settled in France in 1676. At this time he invented 'infinitesimal calculus' which was a revolutionary idea in the field of scientific thought. The well-known scientist Newton also was working on the same subject at that time. Leibniz's paper was published in 1684, and Newton's on 1687. Unfortunately for Leibniz, Newton was selected as the discoverer of 'infinitesimal calculus'.

From Paris he went to Hague where he met Spinoza, and was attracted by his philosophy. He was quite influenced by Spinoza's outlook. From 1673 Leibniz had connections with the Royal family of Hanover and remained in their service for the rest of his life. He became the chief advisor of the Duke of Hanover and was involved in many political activities. He started writing a historical account of the family of Duke of Hanover but before finishing it, he died in 1716 at the age of seventy.

Leibniz was perhaps the "last great philosopher of the Renaissance", commented Prof. Wright in his "History of Modern Philosophy." Leibniz's book "New Essays on Human Understanding" was a revolutionary book in the world of philosophical thinking. As B. Russell puts it: "He was profound, coherent, largely Spinozistic and amazingly logical. His conception of the relativity of space and time, symbolic logic and linguistic analysis revealed his versatile genius". He anticipated, says Copleston, ". . . later symbolic logic." His popular philosophy is found in his book, "Monadology." Some of his other philosophical writings are 'Principles of Nature and Grace,' 'Discourse on Metaphysics'. He established 'Berlin Academy' for higher studies in philosophy and science. In 1700 he was elected the first President of the society of the sciences at Berlin. Leibniz was not only a philosopher, but he was a scientist, historian logician, mathematician, and a religious man too.

II. Leibniz's Philosophy

Leibniz's philosophy can best be understood in comparison with the philosophy of Spinoza. Spinoza was a monist out and out, and the main emphasis in Spinoza had been upon the unity of the world. The factors which Descartes had left separate—mind and matter and God—were all brought together into a unity in Spinoza's philosophy. But the unity, in him, was bought at the cost of diversity and plurality for it was a mere abstract unity which left no place for the reality of individuals. The task which Leibniz took upon himself was to justify the aspects of plurality and diversity. A man of practical affairs, individuals were, to him, indubitably real and no theory which failed to account for their reality seemed to him tenable. A unity must be attained, of course, but it should be unity of the real facts of the world, and not lie beyond them. Leibniz was not satisfied with Spinoza's rejection of teleology or purpose in the world. He advocated teleology, yet at the same time accepted the relative validity of the purely mechanical view of the physical world, with which Descartes had started and which Spinoza tried to justify in his parallelism.

(a) The Idea of Substance

Unity and diversity, teleology and mechanism, necessity and freedom of will—these divergent principles Leibniz attempted to reconcile in his philosophy and the reconciliation was made possible by means of his reconstruction of **the idea of substance**.

Like Descartes and Spinoza, Leibniz based his philosophy on the notion of **substance**. But his substance is different from that of Descartes and Spinoza. Descartes had defined substance as that which exists in and through itself. But if we take independent existence as the criterion of substantiality then the Spinozistic conclusion—there can be only one substance and no diversity anywhere—cannot be avoided.

Leibniz substituted **independent activity** in place of independent existence **as the criterion of substantiality**. Substance is not something passive and inert. It is not that which exists by itself; for then there would be no finite substances, but that which acts by itself. A substance is a being capable of action. Now, with the equation of activity and existence, the substantiality of which the individual things had been deprived by Spinoza, is restored to them. The individual things, though limited, are substantial beings, for they are active.

Descartes had allowed three substances—God, mind, and matter—and had defined matter as extended substance. Leibniz holds that extension cannot be the attribute of substance, for extension involves plurality and can only belong to an aggregate of substances. Each single substance must be unextended. Physicists are right when they regard body as composed of simple indivisible eternal atoms, for every composite consists of simple parts. But they are wrong when they regard the atoms as indivisible, for whatever is material, however small it may be, is still extended and is still divisible. If we are to find a true individisible unit, we are to go back of the extended and material altogether. Matter is thus, at bottom, immaterial. It is made up of substantial units that are themselves unextended. Leibniz calls these units "monads". The monads are both real and **indivisible**. The monads are not only indivisible, they are **immortal** also, for, since they are not composed of parts it is not possible for them to arise and perish through the combination and separation of its parts. The non-spatial or **temporal** character of the monads also implies the impossibility of all external influences. The monads are all **independent** of **one another**, and impervious in nature. No one has any influence over the other. Each monad develops its status from its own inner nature and is sufficient unto itself.

From the immateriality of the monads it follows that the activity in which their very being consists is **spiritual** or **representative activity**. But this representative activity of the monads is not always to be identified with the conscious activity of the human soul. Leibniz draws a distinction between mere representation and conscious representation, between perception and apperception. According to him, below the threshold of our clear consciousness there is a dark background of obscure consciousness, **petite perceptions** or unconscious mental states. Leibniz explains this by means of an example—"The roar we perceive in the vicinity of the sea-beach is composed of the numerous sounds of the single waves. Each single sound is of itself too small to be heard. Nevertheless it must make an impression on us, if only a small one, since otherwise their total, as a sum of nothings, could not be heard. The sensation which the motion of the single wave causes is a weak, confused unconscious perception (**petite perception**), which must be combined with many similar minute sensations in order to be strong and distinct or to rise above the threshold of consciousness. The sound of the single wave is felt but not distinguished, is perceived, but not apperceived*. These obscure states of unconscious representation which are present in the mind of man along with states of clear consciousness—make up, in the lowest grade of existence, the whole life of the monad; there are beings which never rise above the condition of deep sleep or swoon.

The very being of the monads consists in their representative activity. Each monad represents the whole universe within itself. It is a universe in miniature. But the monads are **windowless** and nothing can influence them from outside. Every monad thus is a living mirror which generates the images of things by its own activity or develops them from inner germs. All monads represent the same universe but each one represents it differently, i.e., **from its particular point of view**. Each monad represents that which is near at hand distinctly, and that which is distant, confusedly. Since they all represent the same universe their difference consists only **in the degree** of **clearness**

*Apperception is a perception based on past experiences, that enrich the original perception and add more meaning to it.

with which they **represent**. The clearer the representations of a monad, the more active it is. God alone is 'actuspures' or pure activity and as perfectly clear vision of the universe. All other monads are partly passive, in so far as their perceptions are not clear and distinct. Following Aristotle, Leibniz calls the active principle **"Form"**, the passive **"matter"**, since it is not like God pure form or 'actuspures'. This matter as a constituent does not mean corporeality but only the ground for the arrest of its activity. The principle of passivity in the monad Leibniz calls the **"materia prima"**, and the phenomena of corporeal mass the "materia secunda". The "materia secunda" is the consequent of 'materia prima'—the result of the indistinctness of representation. A group of monads **appear** as a body when it is indistinctly perceived. Matter, thus, is only appearance and not real, for Leibniz. A cluster of monads which are inactive (less active) is perceived as material object or body. The perception of matter, as extended, is illusory or wrong perception. The material world is not real. It is only appearance or phenomena. But though appearance, the perception of extended matter is not without any base or ground. There are an infinite number of monads behind this perception of material things.

(b) According to Leibniz our **perception of space and time also are confused perceptions** of non-existent something. Space and Time are ideal. Space is the idea of monads in the order of co-existence, and time is the idea of order of successions. Monads have no spatial character, they, being conscious atoms, do not occupy space. As Leibniz himself explains it in his 'Philosophical works', "our ideas of space, figure, motion, rest, have their origin in the mind itself, for they are ideas of the pure understanding, which, however, have reference to the external world." Space and Time are relative not absolute. Space is the order of co-existence, and time is the order of succession.* These are abstract ideas of Space and Time. What we perceive as Space and Time in external world is only phenomena, not reality, though this phenomenal perception or illusion has some basis—which is the relation of co-existence (Space), and the relation of succession (of Time). As B. Russell puts it space as it appears to our senses, and as it is assumed in physics, is not real, but it has a real counterpart, namely, the arrangement of the monads in a three—dimensional order according to the point of view from which they mirror their world.

No monad represents the universe just as well as the others; but either better or worse. There are as many different degrees of clearness and distinctness as there are monads. No two monads can be exactly the same. This is Leibniz's doctrine of **Identity of indiscernibles**. There is no qualititative distinction between two monads, but each and every monad is different from every other by its clearness and distinctness of perception, which means there is quantitative distinction among them. Thus, with this principle Leibniz tries to maintain the plurality along with the individuality of finite world of objects. As Leibniz himself observes: "If two individuals are perfectly alike and equal, and, in a word, indistinguishable in themselves, there would be no principle of individuation and that there would be no individual distinction of different individuals under this condition."

*By spatial relations we mean 'above', 'beyond', 'near', 'far' and others similar relations of objects that co-exist. Relation of succession means before, after and similar time-relations.

But though each monad represents the universe differently from others, yet the monads form a series in which the difference between successive monads is infinitely small. There is no gap or break in the universe. The world is a continuous series from the lowest monad to the highest, there being no distinction of kind, but only one of degree. This is Leibniz's **Principle of Continuity**. "Nothing is accomplished all at once . . . Nature makes no leaps: a maxim which I called the Law of Continuity"— says Leibniz.

The two principles—"Identity of Indicernibles' and the Principle of Continuity— Leibniz applies to our actual sensible world but never takes them to be necessary laws. He considers these laws as contingent. Though these two laws are indispensible to explain order and harmoney of this universe, these are not indispensible or necessary for our reason.

(c) Though no two monads are exactly alike, yet the monads can broadly be classified into three types:

(1) the **unconscious** or bare monads: the simple or naked monads stand lowest in the scale. These monads have obscure and unconscious perceptions and pass their lives in swoon or sleep. When perception rises into conscious feeling accompanied by memory then the monad deserves the name of (2) **Soul** and when the soul rises to self-consciousness and reason, or the knowledge of universal truths, it is called (3) **Spirit**. Each higher stage comprehends the lower since even in the spirits many perceptions remain obscure and confused.

From perception arises **appitition**. By appitition is meant the tendency to pass from confused to clear representation. Each monad contains the whole more or less confusedly within itself and by its appitition may rise to a more perfect state. The differences of appitition in the three classes of created monads may be represented as (a) **mere impulse**, (b) **animal instinct** or **blind desire governed by feeling**, and (c) **self-conscious desire** or **will**.

III. Leibriz's Theory of Pre-established Harmoney

The monads form a continuous series from the lowest to the highest. But if the universe consists of an infinity of monads, each independent of the rest, and each containing within itself the principle of all its changes, then change in one monad will destroy the continuity of the series. Each monad differs in infinitely small degree from any other monad. If any change, however small, takes place in the perception or representation of one monad, the continuity of the whole series will be broken and we will have two indiscernible monads. But the change within the monads does take place, it is essential to its nature. The continuous order or system of the monads is destroyed unless we can say that any change within one monad produces or is accompanied by co-relative changes in other monads of such a kind that the equilibrium of the whole system is maintained. This is Leibniz's hypothesis of the **Pre-established Harmony** between substances.

Though no monad can really act upon other monads, yet everything in the universe takes place as if the mutual interruption were real. This harmony has been pre-established by God, the highest monad, at the very beginning of creation. Leibniz never denied efficient cause or mechanical cause in the physical world, but he only says that these causal principles are not applicable in the world of monads. "Each monad is like a subject which virtually contains all its predicates and the primitive force or enteleochy of the monad is the law of its variation and changes. The monads are windowless. There is no causality behind the mutual change in monads,—the change is preestablished by God at the beginning of creation.

(a) Leibniz's View of Mind-Body Relation: This general idea of the Pre-established harmony finds special application in the problem of interaction between **mind and body**. Body and soul are like two clocks so excellently constructed that, without needing to be regulated by each other, they show exactly the same time. Body is not an actual material thing but a group of monads of less developed kind. Every soul or high monad has such a group of inferior associates with which it stands in a specially close connection. The soul follows its own laws, and the body also its own, yet they agree with each other, the harmony between them being pre-established by God. God has "from the beginning formed each of these substances in so perfect, so regular, and so accurate manner that by merely following its own laws which were given to it when it came into being, each substance is yet in harmony with the other just as if there were mutual influence between them or as if God were continually putting hand upon them. Bodies act as if there were no souls, and souls act as if there were no bodies, and both act as if each is influencing the other". As Falkenberg observes: "Over the numberless miracles with which occasionalism burdened the Deity, the one great miracle of the Pre-established harmony has an undeniable advantage".

It may be said that Leibniz tried to reconcile final cause and mechanical cause by his principle of Pre-established harmony. The mechanical explanation of the material world is not denied by Leibniz, he only wants to say that those mechanical laws are based on the Pre-established harmony by God. This is the metaphysical significance of the principle of Pre-established harmony.

But the principle is not satisfactory to philosophers. To say that body and soul agree in their respective state by virtue of Pre-established harmony is to say that a thing is because it is. Moreover, God is here taken as a mechanist who makes a machine with an end in view. But God, who is a perfect being, cannot have an end which He may want to achieve, because this situation makes Him imperfect, God has some end in view means He wants to achieve that goal, and this makes Him limited. The most perfect being cannot have any unachieved goal. Again, Pre-established harmony as a principle explains natural empirical things and events with the help of the supernatural. Besides, his doctrine of Pre-established harmony clashes with his original theory that monads are windowless and they are self-active. If monads are windowless, the law of Pre-established harmony is not applicable on them.

The harmony which governs the universe is a harmony pre-established by God. The monads are created. They are neither absolutely primitive nor the absolute. They depend on a divinity—"the primitive monads are the original simple substance of which all monads are the products and are born from moment to moment by the power of divinity". Hence **we have created monads on the one hand and an**

uncreated monad—the Monad of monads—on the other. The former are finite and relative, the latter is infinite and absolute.

IV. Leibniz's Proofs for the Existence of God

Leibniz gave four proofs for the existence of God: (1) The Ontological or Metaphysical proof; (2) Cosmological proof; (3) Proof from the eternal truths; (4) The argument from Pre-established harmony of God. We will consider these arguments successively:

(1) The ontological argument is also called the metaphysical argument. We pass here from thought of God to the existence of God. Similar argument was put forward by St. Anselm and Descartes, the rationalist.

As Russell observes, the Ontological argument depends upon the distinction between existence and essence. Any ordinary thing or man 'exists' and it or he has certain qualities which make up his essence. In the case of finite things and beings, its essence does not imply existence. But God is defined as the most perfect being. So God as the most perfect being implies existence, on the ground that a Being who possesses all other perfections is better if he exists than if he does not. So the most perfect Being exists.

Kant, however, later, rejected this argument by saying that 'existence' is not a predicate at all.

(2) The cosmological argument is a modified form of causal argument for God's existence. Everything finite has a cause, which in turn had a cause, and so on. This series of previous causes cannot be finite, and the first term in the series must itself be uncaused. There is, therefore, an uncaused cause of everything and this is obviously God.

Leibniz argues that every particular thing in the world is 'contingent', i.e., it is logically possible for it not to exist and this is true of the whole universe. But everything must have a sufficient reason, according to Leibniz, therefore the universe, as a whole, must have a sufficient reason, which must be outside the universe. This sufficient reason is God.

(3) The argument from the eternal truths is that, there are some statements that are sometimes true and sometimes false, e.g., the statement "It is raining". But the statement "2 + 2 = 4" is always true. Those statements that are always true are called 'eternal truths'. Truths are part of the contents of mind and the eternal truths are part of the content of an eternal mind. There must be a reason for the whole contingent world and this reason cannot itself be contingent, but must be found among eternal truths. But a reason for what exists, must exist. Therefore eternal truths must exist and they can only exist as thoughts in God's mind.

(4) The argument from the Pre-established harmony follows from his Monadism. It is an argument from design. This argument shows that our known world is not a product of blind natural forces, but is to be regarded as evidences of beneficent purpose. It is an empirical inference. Though monads are windowless and have no influence from outside, yet we find a harmony in the world. This harmony is established by God, at the time of creation God is the creator of monads, the monad of monads.

But if God be a monad, even the highest and most perfect monad of the system, He would differ from other monads in degree of perfection only. He could not possibly be the creator of the system of monads, because He then would be within the system itself. Leibniz's theology seems to be caught in the horns of a dilemma, either God is a monad and in that case finite beings are not monads in the strict sense of the term, or created beings are monads and then God cannot be called a 'monad'. Leibniz tries to get out of the difficulty by saying that the difficulty in contemplating the absolute simply proves that the human soul is not the monad of monads. "A monadism, if it is to be consistently carried out, must be atheistic, but inconsistently enough, Leibniz believes in both monadism and theism and regards God to be both within and without the system."

V. Leibniz's Conception of the best of all Possible Worlds

There were an infinite number of possible worlds all of which God contemplated before creating the actual world. Out of them all, He chose the world in precisely the form in which we find it. This is Leibniz's famous doctrine of the best of all possible worlds according to which any more-perfect world than the existent world is impossible. It is the best because in this world of ours—which is in space and time—there is everything—here there is good and bad, pleasure and pain, birth and death, virtue and vice. It is only in such a world that man can gradually achieve his desired goal. This world is such that living things can attain perfection through constant effort. The world does not move by mechanical principles alone, the world of living things follow the purposive way of life. Leibniz combines the law of sufficient Reason with the principle of perfection—thus combining the mechanical causation with the final cause. There is a sufficient reason on the part of God while He created this world as the best of all possible worlds. From God's point of view this world is the best of all possible worlds, because here alone the mind has the scope of perfecting itself more and more and make this world a perfect world.

VI. The Problem of Evil

The world that God created, although it contains evil, has a greater surplus of good over evil than any other possible world. In this world there is both good and evil. The question may arise: How to explain Evil? Leibniz classified evil into three heads:

(1) Metaphysical evils, or the imperfection and the finitude of things. This is unavoidable. Created beings without imperfection are inconceivable. This evil is willed unconditionally by God.

(2) Secondly physical evil, e.g., pain, etc. not willed unconditionally by God but only conditionally as in the form of punishment.

(3) Thirdly, moral evil. This evil is permitted by God, for without the bad there cannot be free will and without free will there cannot be any virtue.

At other times Leibniz reduces moral evil to metaphysical evil. The bad is not anything real; it is only absence of perfection; negation and limitation. It plays the same part as shading in painting or disonance in music.

What appears to us as evil is only necessary incident in the life of the whole, which, if we could but see it from the standpoint of the whole, we should recognise as necessary to the highest perfection. We cannot judge an evil by itself. Evil is a negative fact which results from the necessary imperfection and limitation of finite creatures. As B. Russell observes: some great goods are logically bound up with certain evils. In fact, God has permitted evils, because it was only through them that certain higher goods could be brought to pass (Falkenberg).

VII. Leibniz's Theory of Knowledge

Fifty years after Leibniz's date was published his "New Essays on Human Understanding" containing an accute examination of Locke's theory of knowledge.

Leibniz's theory of knowledge may be looked upon as a via-media between the views of Descartes and of Locke. Descartes was a Rationalist, and, according to him, there are some ideas in the mind of man which do not come from the sense. These ideas are present in every mind from the very birth and are self-evident. All knowledge come from pure thought as a logical deduction from these self-evident innate ideas, in complete independence of the senses. Knowledge, according to Descartes, is always analytic.

Locke was an Empiricist out and out and he severly criticised Descartes' position. There are, according to him, no ideas innate in the mind of man. The mind is a "tabula rasa" or a blank sheet of paper at the time of birth and all ideas come from experience.

Leibniz tried to reconcile these two views. As a monad, the soul of man is not, as in Locke's view, purely passive 'tabula rasa', continually receiving external impressions. It is an active force and is the spontaneous source of all its ideas. All its ideas are, therefore, innate. But all the ideas are not clear and distinct from the beginning. The universal truths do not exist already and consciously in the mind at the time of birth. Here Leibniz agrees with Locke in holding that in point of time sensations come first, though these sensations, according to Leibniz, are only confused perceptions or indistinct representations of things external to the individual mind. Universal knowledge is implicitly involved in the sensations themselves, although they are brought to consciousness by the gradual process of clearing up of the original confused sense experiences. The self-evidence of universal and necessary truths is the result of experience, though that experience is purely **internal**. And, though all our ideas are innate, there are many which can never rise to the perfect clearness and distinctions of self-evident truths, but which we have quite a sufficient ground for recognising as true. Further, though our experiences are entirely internal, it is yet objectively real, for it consists in a representation of the whole universe, in accordance with the Pre-established harmony between substances. Human knowledge is thus, at once, a priori and a posteriori, innate and experiential.

In fact, Leibniz's theory of knowledge follows logically from his metaphysics. In metaphysics, Leibniz showed that as a monad our mind is like a universe in miniature. It is self-active, conscious atom which reflects the whole universe within itself. Monads are windowless, so that nothing can act on them from outside. Like a living mirror it generates its ideas from within itself. From this nature of the monad it follows that all its ideas are innate; and all propositions (knowledge) are a priori: universal and necessary.

Leibniz distinguishes between (1) **Truths of Reason,** and (2) **Truths of matters of fact**. (1) Truths of Reason depends on two fundamental laws of thought viz., the law of Contradiction and the law of Identity. All truths of Reason are self-evident and, therefore, necessarily true. Denial of truths of reason leads us to self-contradiction. The proposition "Red flowers are red" is a truth of reason. If we say "Red flowers are not red", we are involved in self-contradiction—which is necessarily false.

(2) But the propositions relating to matters of fact are not necessary, but contingent. The truth or falsity of such propositions depend entirely on the correspondence with facts. This correspondence is known by experience. The truth of such propositions are a posteriori or derived from sense-experience. "Alexander was the pupil of Aristotle"—This proposition is a proposition relating to matter of fact, the denial of which does not result in self-contradiction. The proposition may be false, if it does not correspond to matter of fact reality. It is a **posteriori**, contingent and relative.

Propositions may also be analytic or synthetic. An analytic proposition is one in which the predicate simply analyses the subject, whereas a synthetic proposition is that in which the predicate adds something new to the subject. "All red flowers are red" is an analytic proposition, whereas "all red flowers have five petals", is a synthetic proposition. Analytic propositions are a priori, and, therefore, necessarily true—its denial leads us to self-contradiction. Its truth is self-evident.

All true propositions are analytic for Leibniz. The predicate of an analytic proposition is contained in the subject. All analytic propositions are, thus, self-evident.

VIII. Leibniz's philosophy depends on two fundamental principles: (1) The law of Contradiction and (2) **The Law of Sufficient Reason**. According to him, just as the Truths of Reason depend on the fundamental law of thought viz., Law of contradiction, the Truths of matters of fact depend on the Principle of Sufficient Reason. This principle states that everything has a Sufficient Reason for its existence. "If anything exists, if any event occurs, it must have sufficient reason for its existence."

According to Leibniz all propositions based on experience are existential, contingent, and give us knowledge of this world. The proposition "John Smith married Mary Brown" deals with matters of fact. The denial of such a proposition does not produce self-contradiction. These may be true, may not be true also. Yet, for Leibniz there is a Sufficient Reason behind these facts. If anybody named John Smith or Mary Brown exists—there is, according to Leibniz, a sufficient reason for his or her existence. 'Caesar crossed the Rubicon' is a proposition which tells us about an event of this world of particulars. The truth of such propositions depends on correspondense of knowledge with facts. The law at the basis of such truths is the Law of Sufficient Reason, which states that if anything exists, it must have a Sufficient Reason for its existence. The Principle of Sufficient Reason thus implies that all true propositions are analytic, while the Principle of Contradiction says all analytic propositions are true. The a posteriori or empirically derived propositions also are, according to Leibniz, on the last analysis, can be shown to be analytic and, therefore, self-evident.

Leibniz here distinguishes between finitely analytic propositions and infinitely analytic propositions. According to him, in order to show that the proposition 'Caesar crossed the Rubicon' is analytic, we have to know all facts about the individual man Caesar and, as Copleston observes, "Paradoxical it may appear . . . it is impossible to have knowledge of individuals", because all the facts of the 'complete individual man Caesar' **means infinite number of conditions** which made Caesar arrive at the decision to cross the Rubicon. If anybody knows these all, he will be able to show that the proposition is self-evident or analytic. But, for human intelligence, which is finite, it is not possible for the soul-monad to know all the facts and conditions about Caesar. The proposition "Caesar crossed the Rubicon' is an infinitely analytic proposition. Only God can know such a proposition to be self-evident. We, the finite souls, should remain satisfied with the fact that, these a posteriori knowledge has, at its foundation, the very important Law of Sufficient Reason. In this universe nothing occurs without a sufficient reason for its occurrence. Every event, every occurrence, every fact follows necessarily in a system where harmony is pre-established by God. So all propositions are analytic including the empirically derived ones, because they have sufficient reason for their occurence. [A finitely analytic proposition is that which needs only a **few steps** to show that it is self-evident, and, consequently, analytic. Human mind can prove their analyticity and self-evidence easily.]

In Mathematics and Geometry we find analytic a priori propositions which are necessarily true. But, Physics is a natural science. It deals with the world of our sense-experience. Leibniz holds that as Physics is based on the principle of sufficient reason, it also gives us analytic a priori propositions.

The Notion of Substance, as it Changes in the Hands of the Rationalists

Substance is an important concept for the Rationalists. They identified it with reality. Discussion about the definition, nature, and number of Substance comprises an important part of their philosophy.

Descartes defined Substance as "that which exists by itself, that which requires for its existence the existence of nothing else." In this highest sense only God is Substance. God as the Infinite Substance has the ground of His existence in Himself and is the Absolute Substance. But besides God there are two relative Substances viz., Mind and Matter. Mind and Matter are Substances in the restricted sense of the term. They depend for their existence only upon God but they are independent and different from each other. The attribute or essential property of matter is extension and that of mind is thought. One is the negation of the other. This is the **Dualism** of Descartes. This theory of two kinds of primary substances is responsible for many of Descartes' problems and had a lasting influence in the history of philosophy.

Spinoza found the inconsistency in Descartes' theory of Substance. If by 'Substance' is meant that which depends on nothing else for its existence, then God alone is the substance. Mind and Matter are not Substances because, though they do not depend on each other, they depend on God, the Absolute Substance, for their existence. Spinoza defines Substance, like Descartes, as 'that which exists by itself and is conceived through itself only' and comes to the conclusion, consistently with his definition of Substance, that God alone is Substance. Mind and Matter are not Substances but are attributes of God, the only Substance. Attributes are only different points of view from which the same Substance may be apprehended. Attributes are many, in number, only two—consciousness and extension—are known by human mind. Mind and matter, consciousness and extension, always run parallel to each other. Both are independent of each other. Spinoza, thus, is a Monist, God alone is substance or Reality for him. Everything else is unreal. The universe of finite things and beings—which are nothing but the 'modes' of Infinite Attributes of God—become unreal in the hands of Spinoza. So Spinoza is a **Monist**. God alone is real. Mind and matter are not substances, but are only attributes of One Substance or God.

Leibniz observed that if Descartes' definition of 'Substance' is accepted, then Spinoza's conclusion is inevitable. Spinoza emphasised on the unity of the world. The factors which Descartes had left separate—mind, matter, and God, were all brought together into a unity in Spinoza's philosophy. But the unity, in him, was bought at the cost of diversity and plurality, for it denied the reality of the individuals.

A man of practical affairs, individuals were, to Leibniz, indubitably real and no theory which failed to account for their reality seemed to him tenable. Leibniz substituted **independent activity** in place of **independent existence** as the criterion of Substantiality. Substance is not something passive and inert. It is not that **exists** by itself but that which **acts by itself**. The individual things, though limited, are Substantial beings, for they are active.

He criticised Spinoza by saying that extension cannot be the attribute of Substance, for, extension involves plurality and can only belong to an aggregate of substances. Each single substance must be unextended. Physicists are right when they regard body as composed of simple indivisible eternal atoms, for every composite consists of simple parts. But they are wrong when they regard the atoms as indivisible, for whatever is material, however small it may be, is still extended and is still divisible. If we are to find a true indivisible unit, we are to go back of the extended and material altogether. Matter is thus, at bottom, immaterial. It is made up of substantial units that are themselves unextended. Leibniz calls these units "Monads". These spiritual atoms are the fundamental elements which lie behind every particular thing of the world. Thus each and every individual object is real. This is **Pluralism**, i.e. Not One, but many is real. This is Leibniz's Monadism or Theory of Substance where God is the Monad of monads, the highest monad, other monads are created by Him.

This is how the most important and the most favourite notion of Substance changed in the hands of the three great Rationalists—from Descartes to Leibniz. Unfortunately, however, the Substance' lost its importance in the hands of the Empiricists.

John Locke

(1632-1704)

6

CHAPTER

I. His Life and Works

John Locke was born in 1632, at Rington in England. His father was a Puritan and a local lawyer. Locke entered the Westminster School of Law in 1646, studied there up to 1652. Then he entered the Oxford Christ Church College and passed B.A. and M.A.

He taught in Oxford and studied different subjects which interested him. He had a special fondness for medical science. In 1674 he became a physician, but never practiced regularly. In 1665 he left Oxford and went to Brundenberg where he met Lord Ashley, who was an established politician. Locke took part in English politics of that time, under the influence of Lord Ashlay. Ashlay took active part in the Revolution of 1688 and fled to Holland. He died there. Locke also had to flee to Holland as he had connections with Ashlay. There he studied philosophy and other sciences. In 1689, the Revolution ended and Locke came back to England. He was offered important political posts, but his health did not permit hard work. Locke died in 1704.

Though he lived long, he wrote only a few books, of which his "Essay concerning Human Understanding" was the most famous. He wrote a few books on different Subjects like "Some Thoughts Concerning Education", and "Two Treatises on Government".

He was the founder of the British Empirical School of thought. He was disgusted with contemporary Rationalistic philosophers, who were content with weaving out systems of philosophy out of their own heads. Locke was the first to raise epistemological questions. His "Essay concerning Human Understanding" is an enquiry into the origin, certainty and extent of the faculty of knowledge. According to him, we should first enquire the nature and extent and validity of our knowledge itself. We should know: What knowledge is? How far can it go? Where is the limit of knowledge? Which knowledge is true and which is false? Is the human mind capable of knowing everything? Without getting proper answer to these questions, one should not set forward to discuss philosophical or metaphysical problems like the nature of soul, God, universals, etc. which, according to Locke, was done by the Rationalists before his time.

Locke was always against traditional assumptions, which, he says, takes the place of honest effort in philosophical thought. Locke was like Bacon, in opposing any belief founded on religious authority. He would reject the authority of mind itself if it tried to go beyond its proper limits. He calls himself an under-labourer who clears the ground for master-builders to build upon. Locke regards experience as the sole source of knowledge. But he does not altogether deny the necessity of reason in knowledge. As Falkenberg observes: "Descartes, the rationalist, had despised experience and Bacon, the empiricist, had despised mathematics; but Locke aims to show that while the reason is the instrument of science and demonstration its form, and the realm of knowledge wider than experience, yet this instrument and this form are dependent for their contents on a supply of material from the senses."

II. Locke's Theory of Knowledge

"Locke's Theory of Knowledge is controlled by two tendencies, one native furnished by the Baconian Empiricism, and the other Continental, supplied by the Cartesian question concerning the origin of ideas. Bacon had demanded the closest connection with experience as the condition of fruitful enquiry. Locke supports this commendation of experience by a detailed description of the services which it renders to cognition, viz., by showing that in simple ideas, perception supplies the material for complex ideas and for all the cognitive work of the understanding"—says Falkenberg. In fact it was Bacon who tried to give a systematic form of Empiricism. According to him we should try to attain knowledge of this world with the help of perception and observation, and on the basis of inductive method. The Father of Modern Empiricism John Locke just followed Bacon in his theory of knowledge. His Empiricism is, on the one hand, very rude criticism of Descartes' arguments for the existence of innate ideas in human mind, and, on the other hand, explanation of how, step by step, we can attain knowledge through sensation and introspection (outer and inner experience).

We can find out two aspects in Locke's philosophy—one **negative** and the other **positive**. **On the negative side**, Locke first criticised Descartes' theory of Innate Ideas. He showed that our mind is not born with any idea innate in it. On the positive side Locke proved that all our ideas come from experience—inner and outer.

As an empiricist Locke holds that all our ideas come from experience, i.e., all our ideas are a posteriori. He vigorously opposes Descartes' doctrine of Innate Ideas. Descartes had divided ideas into three classes:

(i) the adventitious, (ii) the fictitious, and (iii) the innate ideas, and held that it is these innate ideas that give us philosophical knowledge. But, according to Locke, there is no idea in the understanding from birth, and all our knowledge comes from adventitious ideals or ideas of sensation.

Locke thinks it necessary to prove that there are no innate ideas. If it can be positively shown that no ideas are innate, then it would be very easy to prove that all our ideas are derived from sense experience. Now, according to Locke, Rationalism is a doctrine which stands on the pillar of Innate Ideas. And if he can prove that no ideas are innate, then the whole superstructure of Rationalism will give way. He has given **several arguments against the doctrine of Innate Ideas.**

III. The Rationalists in general maintain that some ideas must be treated as innate due to their two main characteristics—(i) these are universally present in all minds, and (ii) these are the same in all minds. According to them, ideas of the fundamental laws of thought, some moral principles and the idea of God—these are present in all minds and are same in all minds. Locke's was against this theory of criticism Innate Ideas are:

Firstly, there is no ground on which this doctrine of Innate Ideas is standing. If there were some ideas really imprinted in mind at the time of birth, then these could be easily found out in each and every human being. But we cannot and do not find any idea innate in the minds of children or the idiots or the mad men. They do not know anything about God or Infinitude or the fundamental laws of thought.

Secondly, even if some ideas are found to be accepted universally by all men, we should not be sure as to their innateness. The idea of fire, or the idea of God, which are almost universally present in our minds may be derived from prolonged experience. According to Locke, the fact of general consent would admit of a different explanation "granted that no atheist existed, yet it would not necessarily follow that the universal conviction of the existence of God is innate, for it might have been inferred from the perception of the purposive character of the world", the regularity and order in the external world.

Thirdly, there is no such religious or moral law that is equally present or equally respected in the minds of all men, at all times.

Fourthly, if ideas were innate, then those should be found most clearly in the minds of children, because they have least experience. But, in fact, there is no idea of God or idea of causal relation in the minds of the children.

Fifthly, We cannot also say with Descartes or Leibniz that ideas are in the mind from birth but we were not conscious about them from the beginning. Locke here points out that it is absurd to say that ideas are in the mind, but we are not conscious of them.

Sixthly, Locke argues that if ideas were innate, then we should know them first. If certain propositions are innate, how is it possible that certain other propositions should come before them to suggest the innate ones? It is absurd to call an idea innate if it does not appear in the mind until it is suggested or until a child is able to use his senses. The idea which requires sensation to be discovered cannot be called innate.

Again, if ideas were innate, then we should know them first. But actually this does not happen. Long before a child knows the "Law of Identity" or "the Law of

Contradiction" he comes to know, with his sense organs, that what is white is not black, what is sweet is not bitter. This fact shows that all ideas are derived from sense-experience. The ideas first known are not general axioms and abstract concepts but particular impressions of the senses.

Leibniz thought that all ideas are innate, but these are gradually developed through experience. It is only under suitable circumstances that dormant or innate ideas get fully developed. The innate ideas are often said to be obscure and finally completely extinguished by habit and education etc. Locke refutes this argument by saying that the idea which needs the help of sense experience to make it explicit should rather be called "derived from sense-experience", than innate.

Lastly, it is meaningless, according to Locke, to call an idea innate, when we evidently get it from sense-experience. We can see light by our eyes, hear sound by our ears. These are all derived from sense-experience. Therefore it is needless to call them innate.

Locke fully succeeds in proving that no explicit idea can exist in the mind from birth. **His famous slogan is 'There is nothing in the intellect, that was not previously in the senses".**

IV. Criticism Against Locke's View

Leibniz, however, pointed out that the mind may implicitly or potentially know much more than it is clearly conscious of. Locke failed to ask what is implied in mind's having intelligible experience at all. He himself was constantly speaking of the "capacity of knowing" which belongs to the mind; yet he seems to think that all knowledge whatsoever could be built up out of isolated elements of sense-experience. "There is nothing in the intellect that was not previously in the senses"—said Locke, to which Leibniz added "except the intellect itself."

Man is a rational animal. He possesses a faculty or ability to understand, combine and compare all the raw materials supplied by the sense-organs. This faculty or power is spontaneous for our intellect, so it may be called inborn or innate. The rationalists call knowledge innate only in this sense. That's why, when Locke said **"There is nothing in the intellect that was not previously in the senses."** Leibniz added "except the intellect itself." Again, Locke, to a certain extent, misunderstood Descartes' doctrine. He takes Descartes to mean that there are certain ideas fully formed in the mind at birth which are, therefore, underived from experience. Such ideas are stored up in the mind from birth. But it is unfair to ascribe such an obviously absurd doctrine to Descartes. All that Descartes meant was that mind has an innate faculty of forming such ideas by its native operations without taking recourse to any experience. Thus Locke's criticism does not touch Descartes. It is much later, in 18th century in Kant's philosophy, that we find that experience and reason—both are equally necessary for knowledge. Experience without reason is blind and reason without sense-experience is empty—says Kant. Experience supplies the raw materials of knowledge which make the object of knowledge by the unifying activity of reason. Experience alone cannot give us knowledge.

V. Source of Knowledge—The Positive Side of His Theory of Knowledge

All ideas come from experience. Locke's answer to the question concerning the **origin of ideas** is given in his second book. This part of his philosophy deals with positive answer to the question: How is our knowledge originated? Locke says that Ideas are neither innate in the understanding nor created by the understanding but they are received by the understanding from experience. Mind at birth is a **'tabula** rasa' or like a blank sheet of paper on which nothing has been written. Sensation and Reflection are the only two windows through which the light of ideas penetrates into the dark chamber of the understanding. The perception of external objects is termed sensation, that of internal phenomenon, of the states of the mind-itself—reflection. The child receives ideas of sensation before those of reflection—internal perception presupposes external perception. In this context Falkenberg comments—"In this distinction between sensation and reflection we may recognise an after-effect of the Cartesian dualism between matter and spirit. The antithesis of substances has become a duality in the faculties of perception But while Descartes had so far ascribed precedence to the mind, in that he hailed the self-certitude of the ego to be the highest and clearest of all truths, and the soul to be better known than the body, in Locke the relation of the two was reversed since he made the perception of self-dependent on the precedent perception of external objects".

All original ideas are representations or copies either of the external senses or of internal senses, or of both. **Ideas can be combined by the understanding in various novel ways, but each element of the combination must come through the senses**. It is no more possible for man to create a single new simple idea than to create a single atom of matter.

All knowledge, according to Locke, is based on Ideas. He uses the word in a very wide sense. Usually by ideas we mean the mental copy or image of the perceived object. Plato understood by 'Ideas' the eternal, unchangeable class-essence of things. For him, Ideas are not sensible. But Locke takes the word to mean whatever is perceived or imagined. Whatever is the object of the understanding when a man thinks is an 'Idea'. Ideas exist in the mind. **Knowledge is perception of agreement or disagreement between our ideas**.

VI. Simple and Complex Ideas

Locke divides **ideas** into two broad classes—**simple and complex**. Though the understanding cannot create a single new simple idea, it possesses the power of variously combining those ideas which have come into it from without. The understanding is active though not creative. Understanding is not able to form new simple ideas but it is free to combine them, repeat, and compare them into endless variety of new shapes. Just as a whole language is formed by the various repetitions and combinations of the same letters of the alphabet, so our whole structure of knowledge is composed of the same simple ideas combined in various manner.

(a) Simple Idas: Simple ideas are the elements of thought we passively receive through sensation and reflection. According to Locke, Simple Ideas mostly agree with things, since "the mind . . . can by no means make to itself any simple ideas, these being all the products of things operating on the mind in a natural way." (Book IV, Ch. IV) Thus we can have ideas derived from (a) one sense e.g., taste, smell, colour etc.;

(b) through more than one sense e.g., figure, motion, size etc.;

(c) through reflection e.g., perception;

(d) through sensation and reflection both e.g., pleasure and pain etc.

What is the relation between these ideas and the objects of which they are the ideas? Besides their existence in the mind, Locke holds that **many of the simple ideas are also referred to the external world, where they are supposed to be somehow to belong. Colour, for example, is commonly regarded as, at once, a sensation and attribute of objects**. In order to avoid confusion between the **mental existence of ideas** and **those physical facts which are supposed to give rise to them,** the latter are called not **ideas**, but **qualities**.

In this connection Locke draws an important distinction. According to Locke, **simple ideas are of two kinds**, some are ideas of **primary qualities** which, in reality belong to the object, e.g., ideas of solidity, extension, figure, motion and number. Others are ideas of **secondary qualities** and, in this case, there are no qualities in the object which these ideas resemble. The primary qualities are those that are inseparable from the bodies and are enumerated as solidity, extension, figure, motion and rest, and number. The secondary qualities are all the rest—colour, taste, smell etc. Primary qualities, he maintains, are actually in bodies, secondary qualities, on the contrary, are only in the percipient. Without the eye, there would be no colours, without the ear, no sounds and so on. Secondary qualities are really nothing in the objects themselves but only powers which the objects have to produce various sensations in us by their primary qualities. "Take away the sensation of them; let not the eye see light or colour, nor the ears hear sounds, let the palate not taste, nor the nose smell; and all colour, tastes, odours, and sounds, as they are such particular ideas, vanish and cease and are reduced to their causes, i.e., bulk, figure and motion of parts."

Locke's view is then that the ideas of primary qualities are resemblances of real qualities. These patterns do exist in the bodies themselves. Whereas the ideas we have of secondary qualities bear no resemblance to the bodies, being caused in us by qualities in the bodies which they do not in the least resemble.

[The question here is raised as to how can Locke know that primary qualities belong to matter? Locke simply believes this and accepts it without any criticism. Locke is here accepting the physicists' position and attempts to justify it psychologically. Berkeley shows afterwards that there is no psychological distinction between primary and secondary qualities.]

(b) Complex Ideas: "All our complex ideas of them must be such and such only, as are made up of such simple ones as have been discovered to co-exist in nature." Complex ideas are formed by the mind, by comparing, combining and abstracting from simple ideas. The acts of the mind—wherein it exerts its power over its simple ideas—are mainly three:

(1) Combining several simple ideas into one compound idea.

(2) Bringing two ideas together and setting them by one another so as to take a view of them at once, without uniting them into one, by which it gets all the ideas of relation.

(3) And, thirdly, separating them from all other ideas that accompany them in their real existence. This is called abstraction and, thus, all the general ideas are formed. We might, for example, compare many triangles with each other and, finding that they agree in two attributes alone, we might take only these two attributes disregarding all particularities of the particular triangles. So the general idea of triangle will be a plain figure bounded by three straight lines. Locke's view of general ideas is known as **conceptualism**.

Conceptualism is a theory of universals, in which general words like 'man', 'tree', 'dog', 'bird' etc. have their existence only in human minds. They are nothing but 'concepts' or 'ideas'.

In this context we may discuss, in short, the central metaphysical problem for a philosopher, viz., the Problem of universals. The problem was first introduced into philosophy by Plato. The Platonic view is often called "Realism." Plato held that universals, like 'manhood' cathood, blueness,—really exist. There is this cat, and that cat, but there is also the universal 'cathood' or 'catness'. 'Cathood' is simply the complex set of properties defining cats. But what is the relation, according to Plato, between universals and the particulars? Between, 'man' and 'manness'? They are so different in nature that it would be difficult to see how there could be any relation between them. Particulars like this blue coat, this man—they exist in space and time, and are known by our sense-organs. But the universal blueness which is present in every blue thing is neither in space nor in time. Consequently they cannot be known by our sense-organs. In the world there are many blue things but 'blueness' does not exist in this world, it belongs to the realm of universals. Particulars just imperfectly copy these universals which only really exist, and are known by our understanding or Reason, not by sense-experience. The universals are timeless and unchanging. Even if there is no example of a perfect 'man' anywhere, perfect man-ness exists. They are the realities. This is Plato's theory of universals—known as **Realism**.

Locke's theory of universals is known as "conceptualism". According to conceptualism a universal is not merely a name, nor an image but a **concept**. In reality there are only particulars, but in our minds there is something else—not images but concepts. General words (all words except proper names) are the names of concepts, but these occur in our minds; not in nature. Mind constructs them from the sensible properties of objects. The concept 'man' goes beyond this or that particular man, and seems to be present in all human beings. The individual, particular man is the reality, general name or universal 'man' is a concept, created by human mind. Universals have no real existence.

Complex ideas may be divided into three classes (i) modes, (ii) substances and (iii) relations.

Modes: "Modes are such combinations of simple ideas which do not contain in them the supposition of subsisting by themselves but are considered as dependents on or affections of substances" Modes are those combinations of simple ideas which cannot subsist by themselves, but need a substance or support or substratum in which to subsist.

Modes again are of two types:

1.(a) **Simple modes** are those which are "only variations or different combinations of the same idea without the mixture of any other idea e.g., a dozen or a score, which are nothing but the ideas of so many distinct units added together." Simple modes are, therefore, "contained within the bounds of one simple idea."

(b) **Mixed modes** are composed of simple ideas of several kinds e.g. Beauty, consisting of a certain composition of colour and figure, causing delight in the beholder.

The second complex idea, according to Locke, is the idea of (2) **substance**. Locke thinks that modes are conditions which do not subsist by themselves but have need of a basis or support. They are not conceivable apart from a thing whose states or properties they arc. Substance is the substratum in which the modes inhere. We notice that certain qualities always appear together and habitually refer them to a substance as the ground of their unity in which they subsist, or from which they proceed. Substance denotes the self-existence (we know not what) which has or bear the attributes in itself and which arouses the idea of them in us. All ideas of sensation presuppose a body and all ideas of reflection presuppose a mind. Instead of calling them material and mental substances, Locke calls them cogitative and non-cogitative substances, since it is not inconceivable that the creator may have endowed some material objects also with the capacity of thought.

Starting from the point of view of common sense, Locke is right in arguing that we cannot think of qualities as existing by themselves. Locke's admission of substance, however, is inconsistent with his empirical position. Locke explicitly says that we can have the substance neither from sensation nor from reflection. Yet he never ceases from beleiving that there are substances behind the qualities. It is for him 'the unknown unknowable background of known qualities'. In order to account for the togetherness of qualities, Locke is obliged to introduce the idea of substance, but it remains always a supposition with him.

(3) **The third complex idea is the idea of Relation**. Relations are not copies of actual things but they are formed by comparing and reflecting on things. The understanding in the consideration of anything is not confined to that object merely; it can, as it were, bring one thing and set it by another and carry its view from one thing to the other, the things so brought together (by our understanding) are said to be related.

Types of Relation: (a) **Causal Relation**—According to Locke the experience of change suggests the **idea** of **cause** which brings about the change. Locke is concerned mainly with particular changes and particular causes. He gives no adequate explanation of the Law of Causation as a whole, i.e., the principle "Every event must have a cause". But mere observation of particular changes gives no explanation why every event should necessarily have cause.

(b) **Spatial** and **Temporal Relation:** Objects are always in some space and in sometime, i.e., both in some space and time. 'Far and near', 'in or out', 'above and below' are spatial relations, whereas 'before after, prior to and posterior to' are words that express time relations. Things have spatial relation among them. Events occur in time, and come always one after another. The event which occurs earlier to the other is called prior event, the other event which comes later is called the posterior event. These are temporal relations.

Locke believed in the genetic theory of space and time. According to him, our knowledge of space and time comes from particular experiences of distances and duration. There is some truth in the doctrine, no doubt, for experience is needed to develop our ideas of space and time. But Locke does not see that distance and duration are nothing but parts of space and time so that it is an argument in a circle to derive the ideas of space and time from the experiences of distance and duration. [It is Kant—who comes much later in the history of philosophy—who logically showed that the ideals of space and time are not derived from experience; rather, our experience presupposes the ideas of space and time.]

According to Locke we can set no limit to space or time. The ideas of Immensity and Eternity are, therefore, purely negative ideas. We cannot form any positive idea of immensity and Eternity because they cannot be experienced. To form the complex ideas of an infinite space and an infinite time, we may add together the units of particular spaces and times and stretch them infinitely. Locke, however, does not explain why there should be this mental obligation to go on adding together units of space and time.

VII. Extent and Validity of Knowledge

The Rationalist philosophers before Locke, took it for granted that human mind is capable of knowing everything. It was Locke, the empiricist, who first questioned this attitude.

Locke thinks that he has given a satisfactory account of the way in which we acquire all the knowledge and belief that we have. He claims to have shown that there is no need to believe in innate ideas, since all our knowledge is derived from sense-perception or reflection. Now he proceeds to determine the extent and validity of human knowledge.

Knowledge, according to Locke, is nothing but "the perception of the connection of agreement or disagreement between our ideas." Where this perception is, there is knowledge, and, where it is not, though we may fancy, guess or believe, yet we always come short of knowledge. Truth is "the right joining or separating of signs, i.e., ideas or words." The object of knowledge is, therefore, neither simple ideas nor the relations of ideas to things, but the relation of ideas among themselves.

Locke, here, distinguishes between three grades of knowledge, according to degrees of clarity. Sometimes the mind perceives the agreement or disagreement of two ideas immediately without the intervention of any other idea—this may be called (1) **Intuitive Knowledge**, e.g., that white is not black, that a circle is not a triangle. This kind of knowledge is "the clearest and most certain that human frailty (faculty) is capable of". It is irresistible and "like bright sunshine forces itself immediately to be perceived as soon as ever the mind turns its view that way".

Then the next degree of knowledge is where the mind proceedes to discover the agreement or disagreement of two ideas. This is known as (2) **Demonstrative Knowledge**. Demonstrative knowledge, though certain, is not so easily achieved as intuitive knowledge. Each step in demonstration, however, must have intuitive evidence. Without such perception of agreement there is no new knowledge.

(3) **Sensitive Knowledge:** This knowledge we can have only of those objects which are present to our senses, at a particular moment. Intuitive and demonstrative knowledge are the only kinds of knowledge properly so called. Sensitive knowledge of particular existences only "passes under the name of knowledge". It goes beyond bare probability but does not reach perfection of the foregoing degree of certainty.

We have knowledge of our own existence or Intuitive Knowledge. We perceive it so directly and it is so certainly known that it neither needs nor is capable of any proof.

Of the existence of God we have **demonstrative knowledge**. From the intuitively certain facts of our own existence, the existence of God can be demonstrated. If we exist, something must be in existence capable of producing us. Further, as we possess perception and knowledge, we must suppose that this supreme being who produces us must have intelligence.

Of the existence of material things we have **sensitive knowledge**. Locke admits that this knowledge is not so certain as our knowledge of ourselves and of God. Of the existence of ideas in the mind, we have intuitive knowledge. But whether in any particular case there is, outside our minds, a real object which the idea resembles, is open to doubt, since such an idea may sometimes arise in the mind when no such real object exists. Yet Locke holds that this knowledge, if it fails of being as sure as our knowledge of ourselves and of God, is still practically certain. For nobody can, in earnest, be so sceptical as to be uncertain of those things which he sees and feels. This is confirmed by various arguments. It is claimed that these perceptions are produced in us by external causes affecting our senses because, those to whom any organ is lacking, never have the ideas belonging to that sense.

VIII. Truth

Locke realises that if our knowledge is solely confined within our ideas, then it would be purely subjective and no objective knowledge would be possible. So he is bound to admit that **truth of our knowledge consists in its agreement with facts outside**. **Truth, for Locke,** is **correspondence between our ideas and things outside**. If I see a snake in a rope, my knowledge of the snake is false, but if I perceive the rope just as a piece of rope, then my knowledge of rope is true. The idea of snake in a rope, does not correspond to the thing outside, viz., rope. So it is false. Thus, though knowledge is just finding out agreement or disagreement among ideas, truth or falsity of knowledge goes beyond the ideas.

If knowledge is only the perception of the connection between our own ideas, it would become purely subjective. So Locke speaks of the conformity of our ideas with the reality of things.

But how are we to know whether an idea agrees with an object or not? We know, according to Locke, nothing beyond our ideas.

Locke avoids this difficulty rather easily. He says, **the extent of our knowledge is very limited** for our knowledge reaches no further than our ideas and the possibility of perceiving their agreement. Many things exist of which we have either no ideas, or have ideas which are imperfect. Moreover, we have many ideas, of which we cannot perceive inter-connections. Our ignorance, thus, is greater than our knowledge.

Criticism of Locke's View

Locke is called the founder of Epistemology and the forerunner of Kant and his 'Essay' is often called the English "Critique of Pure Reason". This is his most important book, and the one upon which his fame most securely rests. Locke's doctrine of the dualism between Primary and Secondary qualities dominated practical physics until the rise of the quantum theory in our own day. The theory that the physical world consists only of matter in motion was the basis of the accepted theories of sound, heat, light and electricity. "Pragmatically, the theory was useful," says B. Russell, "however mistaken it may have been theoretically. This is typical of Locke's doctrines."

As B. Russell puts it "A characteristic of Locke is lack of dogmatism. He held that a rational man will support his opinions with some measure of doubt. Thus, in the end, reason reigns supreme."

According to him, reason does not consist in syllogistic reasoning—rather it consists of two parts: first an enquiry as to what things we know with certainty, second, an investigation of propositions which it is wise to accept in practice.

(1) His procedure towards the problem of knowledge, is a genetic study. He failed to ask the central question of Epistemology: How is knowledge possible? This negligence leads Locke to the fallacy that "Sensations alone can give us knowledge." He imagines that the whole structure of knowledge can be built up merely by adding together the particular atoms of sensations. It is Kant who pointed out that our knowledge begins with experience but all our knowledge do not come from experience. Kant pointed out that, though we may not have innate ideas, it does not mean that all knowledge must come from experience. There are some synthetic principles of knowledge (categories) which cannot be derived from experience, yet, without which, knowledge is impossible.

(2) Again, Locke proclaims that our knowledge extends no further than our ideas and that truth consists in agreement of ideas among themselves and not with things. But, inconsistently enough, he maintains that we know, if not the inner constitution, yet some qualities and powers of their existence (primary qualities). Against this it is to be said that there are no primary qualities or qualities which exist both without as well as within us.

(3) Locke maintains that mind is inactive when it receives ideas but becomes active later while comparing, combining, and transforming them to newer and newer

ideas. He ascribed active power to spirits, not to matter, but, at the same time, he had made the former affected by the latter. If external sense is to mean capacity for having ideas occasioned by the action of external material things, then there is no external sense.

(4) A third point, wherein Locke had not gone enough for his successor, concerned the favourite English doctrine 'Nominalism'. Locke maintains that reality is individual and that universals exist only in abstracting understanding. Berkeley brings in the question of possibility of even abstract ideas. The word 'man' means not this or that particular man, it means all human beings of past, present and future. Such a man is never known by sense-experience.

In his "Essay" Locke explicitly says that general ideas are the inventions . . . of the understanding. We compare several individual objects of a class and give a name to their common qualities. This is how the general idea or abstract idea is formed. There is nothing called 'universal,' or 'general characteristic in nature'. These are only names given by us. This, however, is an extreme nominalist position on universals. "All things that exist are particulars, but we can frame general ideas, such as 'man', that are applicable to many individuals, and to these general ideas we can give names" (B. Russell). General ideas have no existence out there in space, yet, in our minds, they exist as concepts. The universal idea "man" is a concept, existing in our minds only. This theory is known as **conceptualism**.

Berkeley criticises Locke's Conceptualism from empirical standpoint and is more consistent in his view. According to him, we never get a universal or general idea in our experience. All ideas are particular, because they are derived from sense-experience. In reality, there is no "man in general; but only" this man or 'that man'. We use the idea 'man' only as a representative idea, representing all men of past, present and future. This is convenient for our thinking. These concepts, according to Berkeley, have not even mental existence. These are only names, which are applicable to all the members of a particular class. They stand for classes, or represent them only. This theory of general ideas which are abstract is known as "Nominalism."

(5) As Morris[1] puts it: "Locke shows that the really vital step on the road to knowledge is the discovery of a necessary connection between our ideas. Since it is this step which distinguishes true knowledge from mere belief." But necessary connection cannot be known by sense-experience. Experience can give us only probable knowledge, may be of a very high degree of probability, but no necessity. Locke here adopts the rationalistic attitude and gives up empiricism.

(6) Again, Locke, in spite of his empirical position, admits the existence of conscious mind, the unconscious material object, and even the existence of God. None of these objects we get by experience. Here we find the influence of the rationalists, specially of Descartes. As Falkenberg puts it: "Locke may not only be termed a Baconian with Cartesian leaning, but a Cartesian influenced by Bacon."[2]

[1] Locke, Berkley and Hume—Morris

[2] Falkenberg: History of Philosophy

(7) Locke recognised Geometrical propositions as universal propositions and as having (demonstrative) certainty. Thus, though he was an empiricist, he tried, as if, to bridge over the gap between rationalism and empiricism, and closely approaching Kant.

(8) Locke, in his theory of knowledge, contradicts his own theory of ideas. As an empiricist he should advocate sensitive experience as the only source of knowledge, but he admitted intuitive knowledge and demonstrative knowledge as more reliable than sensitive knowledge. Here again, we find the cartesian influence on Locke and thus Locke becomes inconsistent.

IX. Locke's Representative Realism

Locke in his "Essay concerning Human Understanding" tried "to enquire into the origin, certainty and extent of human knowledge together with the grounds and degrees of Belief, Opinion and Assent" (B. Russell, History of Western Philosophy). This is 'Epistemology'—a philosophical study of the very nature of "Knowledge" itself.

[In his theory of knowledge, Locke first criticised the doctrine of Innate ideas, advocated by his predecessors, who were mostly rationalists, like Descartes and Leibniz.

After rejecting Innate ideas Locke starts to establish his doctrine of knowledge, which is Empiricism. According to him 'sense-experience' is the only source of knowledge. Our inner experience of different mental states like thought, doubt, attention give us the concept of soul substance, and our outer experiences of sensation, perception etc. give us the notion of material substance.]

In the knowledge situation there is always a subject who knows and an object which is known. Soul substance or mind is **cogitative**, i.e., able to know the object, and matter or material substance is **non-cogitative**.

According to Locke, the mind cannot know the material object directly. Ideas come in between the mind (knower) and the matter (known). Ideas are, according to Locke, the most fundamental elements of knowledge. These are **nothing but the copies in the mind of the real things existing outside.** [Two types of ideas are there: Simple and Complex. Simple ideas again may be of two types: (1) Ideas of Primary qualities and (2) Ideas of Secondary qualities. Ideas of primary qualities like extension, shape, size, motion etc. really belong to the material object. As ideas these are copies of qualities of objects, and enter into the mind from the bodies outside. Mind passively receives these simple ideas. Though the ideas of secondary qualities have their origin in the object, the object does not possess them as qualities but only as a source of power to produce secondary qualities like colour, taste, smell, etc. in the mind. These ideas enter into the mind only under certain physical (external) conditions, and conditions of the knower's sense organs.] Sensation and reflection are the two windows through which the light of Ideas penetrate into the dark chamber of mind.

[Now, at this stage, after passively receiving simple ideas, mind becomes active and builds complex ideas, amongst which the idea of Substance is the most important.

Substance is something existing really behind and beyond the qualities. Substance is the substratum which holds together all the qualities. But it is unknown and unknowable because we never have any experience of the substance—outer or inner. We only know the qualities of a substance (e.g., sugar) like the sweetness, hardness, cubic structure, its solubility in water etc. but we cannot know the substance 'sugar' apart from the qualities. Mind substance is also unknown and unknowable. We infer its existence from different mental states like pleasure, pain, sensation, perception etc.

Thus Locke believes, though inconsistently enough with his empirical standpoint, in both the (1) mind substance behind different mental states and processes; and the (2) material substance behind all its sensible qualities.

This is Epistemological Realism. Locke believes in the real existence of both mind and matter—the subject and object of knowledge. But for him **the subject does not and cannot know the object directly**. The ideas intervene. Mind is confined to its own ideas only—"Knowledge is right joining and separating of ideas". Ideas are copies of objects. The subject knows the objects through the ideas. Ideas represent the really existent objects. Thus knowledge is indirect. The knower does not know the object directly.

The problem here arises: How do we know that my knowledge is right or wrong? Truth of knowledge, for Locke, is correspondence between our ideas with real things outside. If I see a snake in a rope, my knowledge "This is a snake", is false, but if I perceive the rope as a rope—"This is a rope"—then my knowledge is true. Thus, though knowledge is just "finding out agreement or disagreement among ideas", truth or falsity of knowledge goes beyond the ideas. [He mentions: knowledge is **right** joining and separating ideas.]

But it is impossible from Locke's point of view to know the real correspondence between ideas and things. Because 'substance is unknown and unknowable' and mind is confined within the world of ideas. This inconsistency is inherent in Locke's Empiricism which often leans towards Rationalism.

Locke's theory of knowledge is often called Representative Realism. It is **realism** because it admits the real existence of mind, the knower, and matter, the known object. It is Representative Realism because the ideas, through which the object of knowledge is known, are **copies** or **representations** of the object. The mind-substance cannot know the material substance **directly**. It knows it through the intervention of Ideas. Mind directly knows only the **Ideas**, which **are representations** or **copies** of **objects** and their qualities. Hence it is **Representative Realism**.

Thus Locke's Empiricism leads Realism smoothly to Idealism. His distinction between primary and secondary qualities, though supported by contemporary science and common sense, has not been accepted by Berkeley. Berkeley observes that if secondary qualities are subjective because they vary from individual to individual and depend mostly on the position of the knower, his sense-organs, on light and other physical conditions, primary qualities also vary from individual to individual depends on his position, his sense organs etc. A round coin looks oval, even linear from different points of view—even weight and motion etc. depend on the subject. So this distinction cannot be maintained. Either all qualities are objective, or all are subjective. Both depend on our sense experience, so neither of them represent the real character of the object. Matter, if unknown and unknowable, does not exist.

In fact Locke, in his Representative Realism, puts an iron-curtain between the subject and object, making mind confined only to its ideas, and object of knowledge unknown and unknowable. This, ultimately, makes knowledge impossible. Either he should say 'ideas' are the only realities and there is nothing behind and beyond ideas, or he should say that our mind can know the object or substance directly. The first alternative would lead his Empiricism to Idealism at the cost of his Realism, the second alternative would make him an empiricist who cannot avoid Rationalistic attitude towards reality.

George Berkeley
(1685-1753)

7

CHAPTER

I. His Life and Works

Berkeley was born in Ireland in 1685. He was an Irishman. He entered the Dublin University in 1700 where Locke's Essay was the centre of philosophical interest. He became a Fellow of Trinity College, Dublin, at the age of twenty two. From this year he started writing. When he was 28, he almost completed his important writings, which established him as an important thinker in the history of western philosophy. In 1713 he went to London where he met Malebranche and other famous personalities of that time. He travelled to France and Italy also. He tried his best to establish a college in Bermuda, an island, to educate the native American people residing in the island and preach Christianity there. The British Government promised to sponsor the project. But the project did not mature. Berkeley was disappointed and came back to Ireland in 1734. In that year he became the Bishop of Cloyne in South Ireland. In 1752 he went to Oxford. He died in 1753 in Oxford.

Berkeley was famous for his humility, innocence, as well as for his understanding. As C. R. Morris observes, he was one of the most perfect characters among men of letters.

He thought from an early date that a modification of Locke's view is needed for the interest of religion and morals. All his best works were done while he was quite young. "A New Theory of Vision" in 1709, " The Principles of Human Knowledge"— in 1710, and the "Dialogues of Hylas and Philonous" in 1713.

II. Berkeley is related to Locke as Spinoza to Descartes, observes Falkenberg. "It is an irony of fate that a philosopher whose chief aim was the refutation of scepticism, should himself have come to be regarded as simply a link in the chain of sceptical reasoning connecting Locke with Hume, so that Berkeley is simply an incomplete Hume, and Hume simply a Berkeley who has learned the implications of his philosophy" (Seth P. 124).

Locke's conclusions seemed to Berkeley to open the way to scepticism. Locke had postulated the existence of matter but it is only a mysterious substance about which we know nothing. Berkeley believes such scepticism to be wrong because such a view leads philosophy to atheism but, at the same time, he shares Locke's starting point and his business was to show how from Locke's premises (i.e. experience is the only source of knowledge) one may arrive at a different conclusion (i.e. subjective idealism).

Berkeley agrees with Locke in his theory that human knowledge consists of ideas either of sense or of memory or of imagination. But, unlike Locke, he concludes from this that the various sensations or ideas imprinted on the mind cannot exist except in a mind which perceives them.

"Berkeley looks on the refutation of the two fundamental mistakes of Locke,—(1) the assumption of general ideas in the mind, and (2) the belief in existence of a material world outside—as his life work."

III. No Abstract General Ideas

(1) According to Locke, 'all things that exist are particulars, but we can frame general ideas, such as 'man', 'cow', 'tree', without which we cannot communicate our thought. These general ideas are applicable to many particulars, and to these general ideas we give names. Their generality consists solely in the fact that they are, or may be, applicable to a variety of particular things, 'in their own being, as **ideas** in our minds, they are just as **particular** as everything else that exists.' (B. Russell, History of Western Philosophy, p. 610).

General words are different from proper names, like John or Fido, which refer only to particular objects or things. These names are images of the object. But the general words like 'colour' or 'tree' or 'man' refer to each and every member of a certain class. The word 'man' refers to any and every man. In spite of this individual difference in qualities and characters, men are believed to possess some general character, which are common and essential to that class—'man'. The general word 'man' implies the class-character, of human beings.

Locke believed that the general idea of 'man' is an image of this general character—a product of mental abstraction. Mind **observes and compares** several individuals of a class and finds some qualities to be **common and essential**, viz., animality and rationality, in case of 'man'. Then it **abstracts** those qualities from the individuals and puts them under one **name** like 'man', or 'free' etc. So general ideas are abstract ideas, not concrete. These ideas have only mental existence; are abstract, though not empty. We can never perceive 'manners' in a particular man, or 'blueness' in a particular blue object. General idea is a construction of mind. These are present only in the mind or the subject as concepts or ideas. Hence Locke's theory of general ideas is called **conceptualism**.

Berkeley shows that it is not justified to admit of general ideas from empiric standpoint. Berkeley here is a more consistent empiricist than Locke. In his "Princ ples of Knowledge" Berkeley said, "The idea of man that I can frame to myself mu be either of a white or a black, or a tawny, a straight or a crooked, a tall or a low o middle-sized man. I cannot, by any effort of thought, conceive the abstract 'ide Whenever we try to form an idea of colour in general, I have the image of son particular colour, like blue, or yellow or red. I cannot frame an image of colour whi is neither blue, nor red nor yellow, yet it is at the same time all.

There is no general property in particular objects, and no general idea universal corresponding to that property, yet we can treat the 'image' as a gener idea, forget its particularities and take it as **representing** all individuals of a partic lar class. "An idea which, considered in itself, is particular, becomes general by bei made to represent or stand for all other particulars of the same sort."*

By **abstract general ideas** Berkeley refers to such terms as 'triangle' or 'colou or any such general idea and he argues that there cannot really be such ideas. **W cannot really think of a general idea of a triangle. Our idea**, if we examine, **always of a particular kind of triangle**. Similarly, **an idea of colour in gener cannot be formed**. It must be of some particular colour. We may, for some particul purpose, treat our idea of a triangle as representing not one triangle but all triangle we may pay attention only to those aspects of it which are common to it and oth triangles. But, rightly speaking, it is a particular idea. It is better to call it not a abstract idea but a **representative idea**. The only ideas which exist are ultimate particular ideas (images) with a content derived from sense. Such an idea, therefor of "matter", is quite meaningless or rather quite an impossible idea. The general wo matter 'means all material objects of the world. Separate it from particular sensatio and there is nothing left at all. The world that we live in is a world of particul sensations.

Rejection of 'Matter' as a General Idea

Berkeley thinks that Locke's fallacy of material substance arises from his doctrine o abstract ideas; which, according to Berkeley, is an absurd doctrine. For Berkele abstract general ideas are nothing but **names**. This is Nominalism. Berkeley denie abstract general ideas in order to refute 'matter' as a reality exists out there, in spac

It may be said in criticism to Berkeley's nominalism that if there is really n general idea, then we cannot say that an image of 'triangle' stands for, or represen the whole class "triangle". In fact our thought proceeds on the basis of general idea not on the basis of images of particular things.

IV. Berkeley's Arguments Against the Distinction between Primary an Secondary Qualities

Modern Psychology demands that an idea is different from an image, in the sense th an idea is image and its meaning. Image is particular, the meaning or significance o that image is universal. When we think of colour, the image of red may be there, bu

*Berkeley—'Principles'

er and above the image there is something else, i.e. its meaning or significance ıich leads us to the general idea of 'colour'.

Berkeley's argument against matter is most persuasively set forth in his book "The alogues of Hylas and Philonous". The characters in the dialogues are two: Hylas, ıo stands for scientifically educated common sense, and Philonous, who is Berkeley. ›rkeley criticises and rejects **Locke's distinction between primary and second-y qualities of things or substances**.

The primary qualities of an object are those qualities it has "in-itself" quite apart ›m any perception, qualities, it would have even if there were no sentient being to rceive them. These are, in general, the qualities that can be dealt with in science— ›se that can be measured, e.g. size, shape, weight. These qualities are intrinsic to › object. But there are also secondary qualities such as colour, taste, smell and ›tile qualities. The colour that an object appears to have varies considerably. It pends on the light, but also on the condition of the observer: a colour-blind person ll not perceive certain colours at all. Blood looks red, but look at it through a .croscope and it looks transparent with a few red flacks.

The same kind of observation can be made regarding smell, taste and tactile quali-s. A cup of tea will taste sweeter if you have just eaten something sour than it will .er eating cookies.

Locke declared that colour, smell, taste are not qualities inherent in a thing but are ly "ideas" in us, produced by the **secondary qualities** of the object. **The object ›es not possess these qualities but has only a power to produce in the perceiver rtain sense-experiences**. Objects which we call red have no redness themselves: ›y have only the **power** to produce in us the sense-experience we call 'red'. Power in the object, but the 'red' only as idea, is in our minds.

But, the **primary qualities**, according to Locke, **belong to the objects them-lves**. The relation between these primary qualities and the object that cause them is › relation of **resemblance**; an object is really round, and looks round. **Our sense-periences resemble the actually existing primary qualities in the object**. Ac-rding to Locke, Primary qualities differ from the secondary qualities in some very portant ways. They **resemble** the real object behind these qualities, they are **in-parable** from the real objects, they **do not vary** from subject to subject under 'ferent conditions.

Berkeley believed that there is no basis for holding a distinction between pri-ary and secondary qualities. His arguments are:

Secondary qualities like colour, taste smell etc. are **inseparable** from the pri-ary qualities. Colour and shape are inseparable. Shape is simply the boundary of lour. We cannot imagine colour without shape and shape without colour. If the ject does not have the one (secondary quality), it cannot have the other (primary ality).

Berkeley's second argument is that both secondary and primary qualities are **vari-le**. Just as colour varies under different conditions of light and the internal condi-n of the observer, the shape, size etc. also vary depending on one's distance from the object. A coin is round from a perpendicular and is elliptical from an angle; a thing is larger when seen from three feet away than from ten feet away, and so on.

Thus, if variability of an object's appearance under varying conditions of perception proves that the object does not have a certain quality, then **all** the qualities we perceive must be denied of the object and not just the secondary qualities.

Locke proclaimed that the ideas of primary qualities are **resemblances** of these same qualities in the object. Berkeley now says how could we ever know that our experiences of primary qualities resemble those qualities in the object? **"An idea can resemble nothing but another idea"**—says Berkeley. Even if the primary qualities did resemble the ideas of primary qualities in us, nobody can ever **know** that they do.

Again, Locke had admitted that mind knows directly only its own ideas. Then it is not possible for the mind to know whether the objects cause them (ideas) or not. John Hospers here comments on Locke's position by saying that "if you are acquainted only with your own sensations, you cannot smuggle in something which is **not** sensation in order to prove that something other than sensations exists to cause the sensations." (An Introduction to Philosophical Analysis)

Locke claimed that our knowledge of reality consists of ideas and is, therefore mind-dependent. But he (Locke) had at the same time recognised a non-ideal and independent aspect of reality and had distinguished the secondary qualities—as merely ideal—from the primary qualities as having both an ideal and real or independent existence. This inconsistency leads his philosophy to scepticism. The distinction between the ideas and real things makes real knowledge impossible and leads inevitably to scepticism since, in that case, relations of ideas to one another only can be known never the relation of ideas to things. Locke had himself admitted that the secondary qualities exist only in the mind that perceives them. The same reasons ought to have led him to see that the so-called primary qualities are also exclusively mental.

Primary and secondary qualities cannot be distinguished. If we take away all qualities from a thing, absolutely nothing remains. Our ideas are not merely the only objects of knowledge, but also the only existing things—"Nothing exists except minds and their ideas". Sensible qualities' (sweetness, whiteness) are subjective states of the soul substance: sense objects, (sugar) 'sensation-complexes'. This is Berkeley's conclusion.

And this is subjective idealism. Berkeley is known in history of philosophy as Subjective Idealist.

Idealism is the doctrine which holds that 'ideas' are the only realities. The subjective idealist believes infinite Minds and their ideas to be the only realities, while objective idealism believes in an infinite mind whose ideas alone are real.

V. Berkeley Against Locke's "Substance"

Berkeley takes full advantage of Locke's hesitating beginning about substance. Substance, for Locke, is "that which we know not what." "It is the unknown and unknowable substratum of known qualities'. Berkeley thinks that the idea of substance is an unreal and a purely negative idea. Substance is not necessary for the support of the ideas, for ideas cannot exist except in a mind which perceives them

Berkeley comes to the conclusion that the various sensations and ideas cannot exist except in a mind which perceives them. He holds that we really mean nothing more than this by the term "Exists"—"The table I write on, I say 'exists', that is to say, I see it, and feel it and if I were out of my study, I might perceive it or some other spirit does actually perceive it". Berkeley's famous dictun is **"Esse est pericipii" to be, is to be perceived.** In other words, what the ordinary man means by the 'table' is a sensible fact and not a 'table in itself'. "All the choir of heaven and furniture of the earth, in a word, all those objects which compose the mighty frame of the world, have not any subsistence without mind. **Their being is to be perceived, or known.**"

"Suppose matter did exist. How are you going to know that it exists? How can you compare anything besides your own ideas"? The experiment is one that contradicts itself. You try to imagine things existing when no consciousness is there at all and all the while you are thinking of them yourselves. You can contemplate nothing other than your own ideas.

As Hocking puts it: "According to Berkeley our metaphysical difficulties are made by ourselves. We have first raised the dust, and then complaining "we cannot see". To avoid this difficulty he denies the existence of matter and maintains that the existence of things must be determined by perception or **idea.**" As we have discussed before, Locke's fallacy of material substance arises from his doctrine of Abstract Ideas, which, according to Berkeley, is an absurd doctrine. By **abstract ideas** Berkeley refers to such terms as 'humanity' or 'triangle', 'colour' or any such general idea and he argues that there cannot really be such ideas. We cannot really think of a general idea of a 'triangle'. Our idea, if we examine, is always of a particular kind of triangle.

Similarly an idea of colour in general cannot be termed, it must be an idea of some particular colour. It is true that we may, for some particular purpose, treat our idea of a triangle as representing not one triangle but all triangles. We may pay attention only to those aspects of it which are common to it and other triangles. But, rightly speaking it is a particular idea. It is better to call it not an abstract idea but **a representative idea**. The only ideas which exist are ultimately particular ideas with a content derived from sensation. **Such an idea, therefore, as of "matter"** which **belongs to all material objects according to Locke, is quite meaningless or, rather, quite impossible idea.** Separate it from all particular sensations and there is nothing left at all. The world that we live in is a world of particular sensations. The abstract idea of 'matter' is impossible—its being consists in the sensations which we experience in its presence.

Space or extension is the essential quality of matter. Berkeley refutes space as an entity—thus rejecting the essential character of matter. According to him, the so-called knowledge of space comes from visual and tactual signs, and these signs, being sensations, cannot exist outside the mind. The visual and tactual ideas are quite distinct and there is no reason to suppose that they refer to the same space. Berkeley holds that only objective vision is colour. We do not really see the distance. Distance of things is only an inference from the qualities of sensations. It is only through experience that we learn that certain differences in muscular sensation means that in order to touch the object we shall have to go through more or less movement, i.e. our visual sensations are **signs** of our tactual sensations. The connection is just like that between language and its meaning. The connection appears arbitrary though it works.*

VI. Berkeley's Explanation of the External World, His Subjective Idealism

Is there, then, no reality outside our own fleeting ideas? The two most important characteristics of our sense experience are their

(1) Necessity, and (2) Orderly coherence.

"When in broad daylight I open my eyes, it is not in my power to choose whether I shall see or not, or to determine what particular objects shall present themselves to my view." So sensations have a steadiness, order and coherence. Besides, there are clear differences of quality between the ideas of sense and those of memory and imagination. From these it follows that (1) Firstly, ideas require some cause beyond our own will; (2) Secondly, this cause cannot be an unthinking matter, for, there can be no such thing as unthinking matter; (3) Thirdly, the ideas cannot be the cause of one another, because they are visibly inactive.

Is there then any other reality known to us apart from passive 'ideas'?

In addition to ideas we know ourselves or spirits. We know ourselves by intuition and other finite selves by reasoning from analogy. "We comprehend our own existence by inward feeling or reflection, and that of other spirits by reason"—Principles: Berkeley. As opposed to ideas, a spirit is a substance. "A soul substance or spirit is an active being whose existence consists not in being perceived but in perceiving ideas and thinking." We have a 'notion' of spirit, although we have no idea of it.

The cause of ideas is, therefore, an incorporeal active **substance** or spirit. And since our own 'will' is not equal to the task there must be some other 'will' that produces ideas in us, viz., God. Real causality is thus confined by Berkeley to the activity of conscious spirit and removed from the world of objects altogether "Berkeley, after exempting sense phenomena altogether of real causality, refunded all efficient agencies into spiritual will".

The **cause**, in the sense in which we say that one thing is the cause of another thing, has got some meaning for Berkeley. The connection of ideas does not imply the relation of cause and effect but only that of a mark or sign with the thing signified. The fire which I see is not the cause of the pain suffered upon my approaching it, but the mark that informs me beforehand of it. **God is the sole real cause** but He has laid down certain rules for his own activities in order that we may be able to account for certain occurrences and it is to these observed uniformities of the divine activity that we give the name **"Laws of Nature"**. Strictly speaking, there is no such thing as **"Nature"**. Creation is nothing more than the production of ideas in human spirit, by the activity of the divine spirit.

Thus, instead of saying: "the sun is the cause of heat", we should be more accurate by saying that through visual sensations God announces to us that we shall have experience of a tactual one of heat.

*Berkeley's new theory of vision

The natural or created ideas which God impresses on us are copies of the eternal ideas which He Himself perceives through his creative reason.

The connected whole of divinely produced ideas we call **Nature**, and the constant regularity in this succession the **laws of Nature**.

Berkeley proves the existence of God as cause of our ideas of sensation, which often are involuntary. Berkeley's Subjective Idealism, thus, does not deny the independent, reality of objects, it denies only the possibility of their existing anywhere but in a mind. Nothing can exist without being perceived by some mind or spirit. If I do not perceive the table in next room, somebody else is perceiving it, says Berkeley. If nobody is perceiving it, when the doors and windows of the room are all closed, then, Berkeley would say that the "table exists" as God, who is all-pervading and all powerful spirit, is perceiving it. External objects cannot exist without being perceived. So his dictum is **"Esse ess percipi—existence is perception." Everything exists as objects (Ideas) of some perceiving mind or other.**

VII. Critical Appreciation of Berkeley's Philosophy

As a Subjective Idealist, Berkeley cannot accept God as the cause of all our sense-experience. Berkeley argued against Locke by showing that the unknowability of matter is equivalent to its un-reality. He failed to see that the same argument should lead him to the denial of spiritual substance as well and so to the denial not only of finite selves, but also of God, who is, for Berkeley, the corner-stone of his philosophy. In order to save his subjective idealism from solipsism, Berkeley introduced the hypothesis of Infinite Spirit or God. Berkeley tries to save his position by saying that while there is no reason for believing in the existence of matter, the being of ourselves we evidently know by reflection. "I know or I am conscious of my own being and that I myself are not my ideas but something more—a thinking active principle that perceives, knows, wills and operates upon all the ideas." Spirit is not an idea, and yet it is a necessity of thought, an element of knowledge that we can by no means despise with. It is the only real cause, without which the changes of ideas are unintelligible. The nature of the spirit or that which acts is such that it cannot be itself perceived but only the effects which it produces can be perceived.

In introducing the conception of spirit, Berkeley is unfaithful to his original doctrine that we can have no knowledge without ideas. He says that we have no 'idea' of a spirit, but we have a 'notion' of it in our understanding. Thus it is no longer possible to say that the starting point is justified that we have knowledge only of the ideas. It is now obvious that we have knowledge of ideas as well as of notions. But we have notion of spirits. Why not of other things too? How notions are formed, and in what manner they differ from abstract ideas, Berkeley is unable to explain.

Berkeley here has abandoned pure empiricism and has introduced another source of knowledge besides experience. The fact is that Berkeley was only a partial empiricist. He turns to the empirical outlook on our knowledge of external world but when it comes to spiritual world he is both an **Intuitionist** as well as a **Rationalist**. Intuition is a certain kind of experience in which a conviction of certainty comes upon us quite suddenly.* So far as finite selves are concerned he believes that we know our own selves by intuition and other finite selves by reasoning from analogy. As for God, His existence is a necessary condition for the order and sequence of our sensations of external world, since in the absence of any material substance, there is no other way in which the ordinary working of natural phenomena can be explained. The world of sense-experience is not a mirage or dream or fantasy which we create for ourselves. It is, so to speak, a fantasy or invention of Divine mind who presents it to us in an orderly sequence of events. The existence of material objects does not depend on the finite minds, but depends on God's mind and its activity.

But though the material objects depend for their existence on God, it is not clear how these are necessary for God's mind. As Falkenberg points out: "God is in no way bound to imprint ideas on us always in the same order."

Berkeley's theory rests on the assumption that changes in our ideas demand a cause. But Berkeley does not justify the use he makes of the conceptions of cause and effect, nor does he explain what he means by a cause. He simply assumes that we have knowledge of it in our own activity and, without attempting justification, makes it a universal principle. It is because we recognise instinctively that our world must be a rational whole, and that it would not be so unless things are related together in such an orderly way as causal connection, implies that we interpret the world of our experience with this idea of cause.

Berkeley's argument for the existence of God also has its ground upon the rational necessity of the causal relationship and not upon the empirical fact of change.

Berkeley was in many points more consistent to Locke's premises than Locke himself, e.g., he saw that the distinction between primary and secondary qualities cannot be maintained from the psychological position of Locke. The same arguments by which the secondary qualities were proved to be subjective might be brought forward to prove the subjectivity of the primary qualities. But neither Locke nor Berkeley tried to find out whether this psychological position was the ultimate standpoint or not.

The representative perception suggested and accepted by Locke without criticism was passed on to Berkeley. But Berkeley saw that logically we cannot pass beyond the circle of our own ideas. If we hold that we directly perceive our own ideas and nothing more, then, experience being the sole source of knowledge, we can know nothing more. But neither Locke nor Berkeley could see the false psychology of the initial position. It is absurd to say that we perceive our own ideas, for ideas are what we perceive. The statement that we perceive our own ideas is equivalent to the statement that 'we perceive what we perceive': which is a tautology. Every perception has an objective reference. The knowledge relation necessarily involves an object as well as a subject of knowledge, and ideas are what we know about these objects.

Berkeley's criticism of abstract general ideas was rather ineffective. This was due to the failure of the Lockian School to distinguish between an idea and an image, or, rather due to the false identification of the two. The idea—as understood in modern

*A History of Philosophy—Falkenberg

psychology—may be described as the image and the meaning of the image. When we have the idea of a triangle in our mind, we may have a picture of the triangle or an image in our minds but that is over and above the idea. The idea is the symbol or the significance. The image of triangle must necessarily be particular no doubt, but not their significance or meaning. All that Berkeley succeeds in proving is that the image is particular and it is not possible to form an image of a triangle or a man-in-general. But he can prove nothing against the formation of an abstract idea. Towards the end of his philosophy he even admits that thought is not possible without some sort of abstract and general ideas. He says that a particular idea may stand for a class, but it still remains particular. We forget its particularity for the time being and there is but one step from accepting the formation of a general idea by abstraction.

VIII. Whether Berkeley is a Subjective Idealist or an Objective Idealist?

The theory which holds that consciousness is the only reality and the so-called material objects are dependent for their existence on spirit—finite or infinite—is known as Idealism. Idealism may be of two kinds—Subjective Idealism and Objective Idealism. Subjective idealism holds that material objects are only ideas of finite minds only, they have no independent existence, so that these material objects are real only when we know them. These objects have no existence apart from their relation to our minds. The Objective Idealism, on the other hand, holds that though matter or material objects owe their existence on mind or spirit, yet these are not dependent on finite spirits. The material world is ideas of the Infinite Spirit or God, which depend for their existence on God. We, the finite spirits, cannot produce idea of material objects at our own will. These are out there in space and does not depend on our minds for their existence. But material objects must be objects of some mind, or subject, or spirit-on God's mind, if not ours.

The question often arises as to whether Berkeley's world view is Subjective Idealism or Objective Idealism. As we have seen, in the first part of his philosophy, Berkeley wanted to establish Subjective Idealism. He explicitly stated in the latter part of his philosophy that though the world depends for its existence on consciousness, or mind, it does not depend on finite minds—such a view is evidently Objective Idealism.

But Berkeley is unable to prove the existence of the infinite mind or God from his empirical standpoint. Ideas or objects exist in God's mind, but he could not show, without taking recourse to rationalism, that these ideas are necessary for God also. As Hegel puts it "Just as the world would not be a world without God, similarly God would not be God without a world." There is no such necessary connection between God and the world in Berkeley's idealism. He thus arrives at his Objective Idealism just to escape from **solipcism**.* He brings the conception of Infinite Spirit or God just to show that the world is not a dream or mirage of finite selves. Thus it may be said that Berkeley arrives at Objective Idealism at the cost of his empiricism. It is Hume who consistently carried out Locke's empiricism to Scepticism.

Berkeley's Subjective Idealism has been vehemently criticised by the Neo-Realists like Russell, Perry Moore and others. Their main point of criticism is that Berkeley

*Solipcism is a form of extreme Subjective Idealism, which holds that only 'I' and 'my ideas' exist.

is wrong in thinking that the object of knowledge depends solely fôr its existence on the subject of knowledge. In knowledge-situation, the subject knows the object. **The knowledge of the object** depends on the subject who knows. But this fact does not logically lead us to the conclusion that the object of knowledge depends for its **existence** on the subject. The realists hold that the object can exist independently of the subject. Perry an well-known Realist, criticised Berkeley, which is known as "Ego-Centric Predicament"—an unwanted difficult situation that centres round the ego or the subject.

David Hume
(1711-1776)

8
CHAPTER

I. His Life and Works

David Hume was born on the 26th April 1711, at Edinburgh. His family wanted him to take up the legal profession. But he did not like it. He had a special fondness for literature, arts and Philosophy. In 1748, he published his famous book "Enquiry Concerning Human Understanding." The main publications that followed were Enquiry Concerning the Principles of Morals (1751), Political Discourses (1752), History of England in Six Volumes (1754-62) and Dialogues concerning Natural Religion (1779).

II. Hume's Greatness as a Philosopher

Though Hume's greatness as a philosopher has never been questioned, yet Hume's exact place in the history of philosophy has remained a matter of dispute. Hume is the most consistent empiricist and carries out in his philosophy the sceptical consequences which logically follow from the findings of Locke and Berkeley. Exposed to Hume's criticism, the world of knowledge which Locke had so laboriously constructed disappears altogether and disintegrates into separate and disconnected elements among which there is no bond of union, no principle of organisation. Berkeley had criticised the material substance of Locke but, inconsistently to his empirical position, he maintained spiritual substances to be real. Hume, in his turn, shows the unreality of the spiritual substance as well and reduces both the material and spiritual world into a series of loose disconnected and discrete sensations. So, given Locke's premises, there remains in the final conclusion nothing substantial, systematic or necessary, but merely the fleeting impressions of the moment. Philosophy of Hume is the last word of Empiricism. Here reason is employed to show the weakness of reason, and reason is turned against itself.

This is the traditional interpretation of Hume's Empiricism. But it was Kemp Smith who exposed the baselessness of this criticism against Hume. Hume never wanted to demolish metaphysics like Locke. He also gave much importance to Epistemological discussions in philosophy. Hume analysed the contents of human understanding to show that human mind is not fitted for such abstruse subjects like metaphysics. In fact, Hume wanted to lay the foundation of true metaphysics as distinguished from false and spurious metaphysics. As B. Russell observes, we can see the traces of Rationalism, Empiricism, Phenomenalism, and even linguistic philosophy in his writings.

III. Hume's Impressions and Ideas

Section II of "Enquiry Concerning Human Understanding" introduces Hume's basic empiricistic principle, viz, the principle that "all our ideas or more feeble perceptions are copies of our impressions or more lively ones".

Following the same method as Locke, Hume analysed human knowledge into its constituents and finds that perceptions, i.e., mental states, may be divided into two classes viz, **impressions and ideas**. "The difference between them consists in the degrees of force and liveliness with which they strike upon the mind. Those which enter into mind with more force and violence we may name impressions. . . . By ideas I mean the faint images of these in thinking and reasoning."

"The word 'idea' was already in use, but Hume uses it in a definite sense, defined it, and has introduced a new word 'impression' while defining "idea". The distinction between impressions and ideas is given now in psychological terms, so that the distinction is verifiable in immediate experience". The distinction lies in degree of vivacity, liveliness or intensity. Ideas are defined by Hume as copies of impressions. "By the term **impression** . . . I mean all our more lively perceptions, when we hear or see, or feel or love or hate or will" (Enquiry). When we receive a red object, we have an impression of red, and when the object is removed from my sight, or I close my eyes, I still have a faint image of red in my mind. This is the idea of red. Thus an 'idea' is an **image** or copy of the corresponding impression.

According to Hume we cannot form an idea without a previous impression. A blind man cannot form the idea of red, because he has not the previous impression or perception of 'red'. Hume applies his view on mental experiences also. He who hasn't it the direct experience of pain cannot have the idea of pain, he who has not felt hatred can never have the 'idea' of hatred.

There is considerable difference between an idea and an impression. The most lively thought (idea) is still inferior to the dullest sensation. By the term 'impression' Hume means "all our more lively experiences, when we hear, or see or feel, or love or hate or desire or will." And impressions are distinguished from ideas, which are less lively perceptions, of which we are conscious, when we reflect on any of those sensations. All the materials of thinking are derived either from our outward or inward sensations. "All our ideas or more feeble perceptions are copies of our impressions or more lively ones."

Hume proves this by two arguments:

(a) First, when we analyse our thoughts or ideas, however sublime or complex, we always find that they resolve themselves into such simple ideas as were copied from a precedent feeling or sentiment. When we think of a golden mountain, we only join two ideas, gold and mountain, with which we were acquainted before. We form the idea of God as an infinitely intelligent, wise, powerful, and benevolent personality. Our experience of different moral qualities are infinitely stretched or expanded by our imagination. The creative power of the mind amounts to no more than the faculty of compounding, augmenting, or diminishing the materials afforded to us by the senses. In short, all the materials of thinking are derived from either our outward or inward sensations. The mixture and composition of these belongs alone to the mind and the will.

(b) Secondly, if a man, from a defect of an organ, is not able to have that particular sensation, we always find that he is unable to have the correspondent ideas. A deaf man can form no idea of sound, a blind man can form no idea of colour.

So Hume's conclusion is: No impressions, no ideas. "There is however, one contradictory phenomenon, which may prove that it is not absolutely impossible for ideas to arise independent of their correspondent impression. Suppose a person is perfectly acquainted with colours of all kinds except one particular shade of blue, for instance. Is it possible for him to form the idea of that shade from his imagination? Hume says that he can form the idea of that particular missing shade of blue. But this instance is, for Hume, **so singular** that it cannot alter his general maxim—No impressions, no ideas.

"All ideas, especially abstract ones, are naturally faint, and obscure. The mind has but a slender hold of them. On the contrary, all impressions, that is, all sensations, either outward on inward, are strong and vivid. They are exactly determined, nor is it easy to fall into any error or mistake with regard to them."

"Here then we have", Hume suggests "a method by which many philosophical difficulties might be solved. When we entertain any suspicion that a philosophical term is employed without any meaning or idea (as is but too frequent), we need but enquire from what impression is that supposed idea derived? And if it be impossible to get any, this will serve to confirm our suspicions." **The relation of ideas and impressions is one of derivation of one from the other**. Ultimately all our ideas are derived from impressions are only copies of our impressions. At first sight it may appear that mind has an unbounded liberty in the formation of ideas, that it can form ideas of things of which we have never had any impression. But when carefully examined, it is found that such ideas can always be analysed into elements with which we have always been acquainted by way of impression. "Hume thus avoids the inconsistencies of both Locke and Berkeley. Locke had proposed to start with nothing but ideas yet, for him, each idea carries with it an account of its origin and presented as a quality of some real thing. For Berkeley it is the universal mind which is the background of all our ideas. But the real background of ideas or perceptions, whether material as with Locke, or theological as with Berkeley, is simply wiped out by Hume from his theory." "The difference between impressions and ideas is so evident that there is no scope of any confusion between them. The actual outer or inner sensations may be termed impressions: the weaker images of memory or imagination which they leave behind them—"ideas". Hume uses these words to distinguish the impressions from ideas: Impressions are 'strong', 'forceful', 'lively' and 'vivacious'; ideas are weak, less forceful, less lively, and less clear. The feeblest impression is never confused with the strongest idea. The difference is not only a difference of degree, but they seem to be qualitatively different too. **Since nothing can gain entrance to the soul except through outer and inner sensation, there is no idea which has not arisen from an impression or several such.** Every idea is an image and copy of an impression."

IV. Laws of Association

Ideas do not occur entirely at random but in an orderly connection with each other. There are three laws of association. These are the bonds or connections between ideas, by which one idea revives the other, in our minds. The three laws of association are: (i) Law of Similarity, (ii) Law of Contiguity, and the (iii) Law of Causality. "The three connecting principles of all ideas are the relations of resemblance, contiguity and causation"—says Hume in his 'Enquiry'.

The Law of Similarity says, similar things tend to revive one another. The photograph of a person reminds us of the person. The law of Contiguity or nearness says contiguous things tend to revive one another. Lightning revives in us the idea of thunder. This is contiguity or nearness in time. The name "Gitanjali" reminds us of Rabindranath Tagore. This is continguity in space. The Law of Causality claims that if two events are connected as cause and effect, then one revives the image of the other. Cloud and rain, mosquito bite and malaria are connected by way of the law of causality.

To emphasise the importance of these laws in our everyday experience, Hume compares them to the principle of universal attraction in physics,—says Morris. According to Hume, one idea is associated with another entirely by repeated occurrence. We find in our experience that two ideas go together several times—and these two are associated. Thus Hume thinks that though our mind is confined to its impressions and ideas, which are discrete and disorganised, the laws of association bind these perceptions together and we are able to pass from one idea to another.

But the question here arises as to 'Who is employing the laws of association?' Hume does not believe in a permanent self. So he is unable to answer how the laws are employed or who employs these laws.

Again, all these laws refer to actual objects. As Mohanti observes, the relation of cause and effect obtains amongst objects and their ideas. The actual cloud and rain are causally connected. The idea of cloud is not causally connected with the idea of rain.

Thus Hume only accepts these laws of association and analyses them psychologically.

V. Relations of Ideas and Matters of Fact

Hume thinks that all our objects of knowledge, all objects of enquiry, are of two kinds:

(1) Relations of Ideas, and (2) Matters of Fact. This division reminds us of Leibniz's classification of proposition as Truths of Reason and Truths of Fact.

The science of Geometry, Algebra, and Arithmetic are said to be concerned with relations of ideas. One important characteristic of such knowledge is that, it is 'a priori' or independent of experience. Our knowledge—"Two plus two is equal to four" or "three times five equals to half of thirty" exemplifies relations of ideas. "Propositions of this kind are discoverable by the mere operations of thought, without depending on what is anywhere existent in the universe." says Hume.

The other important characteristic of these 'a priori' propositions is that, the denial of such propositions leads to self-contradiction. We cannot even conceive of the negation of these propositions. "2 + 2 = 4" is an a priori proposition. Its truth does not depend on fact. It is self-evidently true. It is not possible to think that 2 + 2 is not equal to 4. 'A priori' propositions only analyse the whole or part of the subject in the predicate. When we say, 'All men are rational animals'—this proposition is such that we cannot deny it without being involved in self-contradiction. Here the predicate 'rational animal' is nothing but the analysis of the subject term "men", (animality and rationality are the defining characters of man). The predicate in such propositions do not add any new information to the subject term but only analyses it. A priori propositions are analytic.

On the other hand, our knowledge concerning matters of fact is not obtainable by mere operations of reasoning. Such knowledge needs sense-experience. Knowledge like 'water quenches our thirst', or 'my friend has a pet dog' are not necessarily true, but are contingent, i.e. their truth or falsity depend on our experience of the fact. Here the predicate adds some new information to the subject, goes beyond the defining character of the subject term and becomes probable. Such knowledge is not a priori, but "a posteriori", i.e. derived from experience. The denial of these propositions are not self-contradictory, but is only false. "That the sun will not rise tomorrow is no less intelligible a proposition and implies no more contradiction than the affirmation that it will rise". The absolute certainty that is characteristic of our knowledge concerning relations of ideas (mathematical knowledge) is absent here. There is no logical contradiction in thinking that the sun will not rise tomorrow. Such propositions are only probable or contingent, not necessary.

This bilateral division of knowledge by Hume is very important from the point of view of history of philosophy and has a far-reaching influence on philosophers of modern age. The first group of propositions (Relations of Ideas) are "analytic a priori propositions of the Logical Positivists of modern philosophy. On the other hand, the propositions concerning matters of fact are the "Synthetic a posteriori' of the modern Logical Positivists. According to the Logical Positivists metaphysical propositions are neither synthetic 'a posteriori, nor analytic 'a priori'. So metaphysical propositions which deal with supersensible entities like God or Soul, or substance etc. are meaningless. Hume too expressed his antimetaphysical attitude when he said any discussion on such entities are beyond our knowledge and so are to be abandoned. It is in Kant's theory of knowledge that we get a reconciliation between these two types of knowledge. Kant speaks of 'synthetic a priori' propositions which are alone "knowledge" in the truest sense of the term, where both sense-experience and reason have their important contributions.

VI. Hume's View on Causality

The Regularity theory of causal relation—According to Hume, "**all reasonings concerning matters of fact are founded on the relation of cause and effect**. Whenever we want to go beyond our perception or memory, beyond the testimony of our senses and reports of memory—we base our knowledge on cause and effect. A man finding a watch or any other machine in a desert island would conclude that there had once been men in the island: we always suppose in such cases that there is a connection between the present fact and the past fact which we are inferring. Our knowledge of causal relation helps us to pass from known facts to the unknown."

In dealing **with matters of facts**, we can never say that the contradictory is logically impossible. Hume claims that our knowledge of causal relation is not obtained by a priori reasoning. Hume asks the question, how do we know that Alexander had once invaded India? or that last night my house was burgled when I was not at home? We arrive at our conclusion by a process of reasoning and the principle behind these sorts of 'reasoning concerning matters of fact, is the relation of cause and effect'. Hume examines our knowledge of causal relation and tries to find out what degree of certainty belongs to the conviction that all things are connected with other things as cause and effect.

Hume, consistently with his empiricism, searches here for the **'impression' of our idea of causal relation**. As is usual with Hume, he says that if we are unable to find out any such impression, the corresponding 'idea' is unwarranted.

Our knowledge of cause and effect is derived entirely from experience and cannot be derived from 'a priori' reasonings, because, Hume claims, that all judgments of pure reason like '2 + 2 = 4; or 'three times five is equal to half of thirty'—are analytic, whereas causal judgments are synthetic. Being analytic an a priori proposition is necessary, but a causal proposition like 'bread affords nourishment' is probable only, not certain. Here the predicate adds some new character to the subject, which may not be always true. Such a proposition is obtained by experience only.

Again, Hume argues that cause and effect are two different things. No amount of analysis of cause gives us any knowledge of the effect. Cause and effect are entirely independent of each other. If an absolutely new object is given to a man, he will not be able to discover its cause, nor its effect. "Adam," says Hume, "at the very first, could not have inferred from the fluidity and transparency of water that it would suffocate him, or from the light and warmth of fire, that it would consume him... Our reason, unassisted by experience, can never draw any inference concerning matters of fact. Thus causes and effects are discoverable not by reason but by experience."

Repeated experience of two events occurring one after another, in close succession, are imagined to be connected. We start inferring one from the other. Lightning and thunder occur several times in close succession in our experience. We infer, or preferably say expect, the consequent event (thunder) with the appearance of the antecedent event (lightning). This, according to Hume, is the influence of custom. We think that even in future B will occur after A appears. The mind can never possibly find the effect in the supposed cause, because the effect is totally different from the cause. "Motion in the second billiard ball is a quite distinct event from motion in the first, nor is there anything in the one to suggest the smallest hint of the other. There is no a priori or necessary connection between the two."

Every effect, Hume says, is a distinct event from its cause. It could not, therefore, be discovered in the cause. There is nothing in any object, considered in itself, which can afford us a reason for drawing a conclusion beyond it. "We argue that fire will warm us and bread afford nourishment because we have often perceived these causal pairs closely connected in space and time."

But what is the warrant for transforming perceived succession in time into causal succession? Any and every pair of successive events are not looked upon as related by way of causality. It is only when we find in our experience that a certain event follows a certain prior or antecedent event **several times** that we come to believe that these two events are necessarily connected with each other. Belief in causation is therefore, due simply to **custom-born habit of expectation**.

In keeping with this logic **Hume defines a cause as an "object followed by another and where all objects similar to the first are followed by objects similar to the second**."

Cartesian philosophers, and the scholastics believed that causal relation is a relation of necessary connection, like logical connections. Hume first challenged seriously this view. His argument was twofold: (1) First, he showed that causal propositions are not 'a priori, (2) Secondly, he pointed out that there is no 'power' or 'force' in cause, that is usually believed not only by the philosophers but also by the ordinary people.

(1) Hume claims that our knowledge of this relation is not obtained by 'a priori' reasoning. A priori knowledge is independent of experience. The proposition "Three times five is equal to half of thirty" (expressing relation between numbers) is discoverable by the mere operation of thought without dependence on what is anywhere existing in the universe. In such a priori propositions, the predicate only analyses the subject—so it is necessary. Negation of such necessary a priori propositions gives rise to self-contradiction. We cannot even conceive of the negation of a priori propositions. In dealing with matters of facts, however, we can never say that the contradiction of such a posteriori propositions are logically impossible. The sun will rise tomorrow is no less intelligible a proposition and implies no more contradiction than the negation that it will not rise." All a priori propositions are analytic. Here the predicate only analyses the subject. But no amount of analysis of cause can give us any knowledge of the effect. Cause and effect are two entirely different events, independent of each other. There is nothing in any object that can refer to another object. Our reason, unassisted by experience, can never draw any inference concerning real existence and matters of fact. Adam, the first man, could not have inferred from the

fluidity and transparency of water that it would suffocate him, or from the light and warmth of fire, that it would consume him (Enquiry: Hume). "Every effect," Hume says, "is a distinct event from its cause. It could not . . . therefore be discovered in the cause . . . There is nothing in any object considered in itself, which can afford us a reason for drawing a conclusion beyond it." We argue that fire will warm us, and bread afford nourishment because we have often perceived these causal pairs closely connected in space and time. In the case of a phenomenon previously unknown, we cannot tell from what cause it has proceeded, nor what its effect will be.

But even experience does not vouchsafe all that we desire. It shows nothing more than co-existence and succession of phenomenon or events, while the judgment itself, for example, "the motion of one body stands in causal connection with that of another" (or 'bread affords nourishment'), asserts more than mere contiguity in space and time. It affirms not merely that the one precedes the other but that it **produces** it—not merely that the second event follows the first, but that it **results from it**. We believe that the cause has a power to produce the effect. Milk has a 'power' to produce curd.

The bond that connects the two events, the force that puts forth the second from the first, the necessary connection between the two **is not perceived, but is added to perception, by thought, is construed into it.**

(2) Hume had divested causality of all such notions as power or efficacy. The bond which connects cause and effect, the force that puts forth the second from the first, the power that produces the effect from the cause is **not perceived but is added to perception by thought, is construed into it**. What is the warrant for transforming perceived succession in time into causal succession? Any and every pair of successive events are not looked upon as related by way of causality. It is only when we find in our experience that a certain event follows a certain prior or antecedent event **several times** that we come to believe that these two events are necessarily connected with each other. Taking poison is the cause of death. Several times we have seen these two events happening one after another, which helps us to conclude that poison and death are causally connected, that poison has the power of producing death. **Necessary connection or power, therefore, is a product of our imagination**. These ideas are not copies of any corresponding impression of power. **Repeated experience** of two events occuring one after another, in close succession, are imagined to be connected. We start inferring one from the other. Two events, lightning and thunder, occur repeatedly in close succession in our experience. We expect the consequent event with the appearance of the antecedent event. Causality is a custom-born habit of expectation and nothing more. Objects are not connected, but we imagine them to be connected, because they often go together in our experience.

In keeping with this logic Hume defines a cause as "an object followed by another and where all objects similar to the first, are followed by objects similar to the second." Hume's final definition of cause is this "a cause is an object, precedent and contiguous to another and so united with it in the imagination, that the appearance of the one determines the mind to form the idea of the other and the impression of the one to form a more lively idea of the other." **Not necessary connection, but regularity of sequence is the essence of the relation of cause and effect.**

Hume claims that **'power'** or **'force'** that produces effect from the cause is not discoverable by the reflection on the operations of our own minds also. We often feel or are conscious of internal **'power'**. "An act of volition produces motion in our limbs or raises a new idea in our imagination. We think that our will has 'power' enough to produce changes in our limbs." Hume observes that "the motion of our body follows upon the command of our will. But the means by which this is effected, the power 'by which the will operates' for ever escapes our most deligent enquiry."

Hume criticises the commonsense view of **'will-power'** by saying that a man suddenly struck by paralysis often tries to move his limbs, but in vain. Here the cause (will) is present but not its necessary consequent (movement of hand). So power is not inherent in will. All that we perceive in voluntary actions is that our will is followed by a change in our limbs or a change in the external world. The concept of 'power' or 'force' is therefore a non-entity. Two events—one mental and another physical—occur one after the other and we imagine from their regularity of sequence that they are causally connected.

The consciousness of power in ourselves when we produce an effort, was taken by Berkeley as a fact. Hume says that though we have a feeling of effort, still we can find no necessary connection. We only have the feeling of exercising will followed by the idea of some change in the external world.

Thus, Hume searched for the impression of necessary connection or power in causal situation, but failed to discover any. So he concludes that experience, which is the source of all our knowledge, cannot supply us with necessary connection or power. Causal relation involves no power, no necessary connection. It is only regularily of sequence between two events. This much we get in our experience, and, as a strict empiricist, he does not like to add anything else.

Critical Appreciation of Hume's View of Causality

The whole difficulty of Hume in giving a true account of causality arises from his defective view of experience. His theory of **cause as a regular antecedent of the effect** has been criticised vehemently by philosophers from various paints of view.

(1) If Hume's view is accepted we should say that day is the cause of night, because there is a regularity of sequence between these two events. In fact day and night both are caused by the rotation of earth. This is confusing a condition for a cause.

(2) Historical events which have occurred only once cannot be explained by Hume's regularity theory of causation. We think the attack of Poland by Hitler is the cause of the Second World War. But the event occurred only once in history. Regularity theory fails to explain such events.

(3) On the contrary, there are many events that occur regularly one after another yet are not believed to be causally connected e.g. Malaria occurs almost always with fever and trembling of the body. Yet the fever has not been recognised as the cause of Malaria. The cause here is something else, i.e. the biting of a particular kind of mosquito.

(4) As Ewing observes, when I raise my hand as per the command of my will I believe that my will is the cause of raising of my hand. I cannot agree with Hume that it is not controlled by my will but is only a regular sequence of my will.

(5) The exclusion of the idea of power from the notion of cause is also open to question. As Wright remarks "we know the cause as productive of the effect, or we do not know the cause at all."

Lastly, Hume conceived experience to be made up of isolated impressions or ideas and, due to this defective conception of experience itself, he failed to find out any connection between two facts in our experience, which is all that is implied in the conception of 'cause'.

Indeed, Hume looked for causality where it could not be found. Granted the premises the conclusion is inevitable. But in our experience we never get an altogether isolated event. Every particular experience points beyond itself to other particular experiences along with which it forms a system. What we regard as cause and effect are not, therefore, isolated experiences even at the very beginning. They are already bound up with one another. Thus, to establish a necessary connection is not so difficult a task, as Hume imagines.

Like Locke, Hume failed to explain the universality of the demand for cause. The view of cause that Hume leads us to is not that which, as a matter of fact, its generally accepted meaning. We do not merely expect the effect to follow the same cause, we believe that if the conditions be the same, it must do so and it does not need more than one experiment to establish universal causal relation, provided the experiment is perfect. No customary association, but necessary connection, is the essence of the causal relation and there is an element in the latter which the former by no means can explain. Thus we find that Hume's explanation of causal connection is rather an instance of failure to explain.

Moreover Hume attempt to explain particular cases of causal relation like 'a is the cause of b' or "c is the cause of c"—and that also not in keeping with the general use of the term. It is not an explanation of the universal causal law: "Every event must have a cause." It is Kant who took up the thread and explained satisfactorily the universal causal principle as a 'synthetic a priori category' of the understanding.

VII. Humean Explanation of External World

Though we speak as if there are objects existing outside the mind, the fact is that, in reality, it is only our ideas that we can directly perceive or know. And now that Hume has resolved the principle of causation into mere expectation due to custom, there is no way of getting outside those subjective facts of consciousness. The world is merely a complex of sensations. But, then, what causes us to believe in the existence of an independent world of identical things? Why, on the one hand, we attribute continued existence to objects even when they are not presented to the senses? Why, on the other hand, we suppose them to have an existence distinct from the mind? Our knowledge is made up of impressions and in the impressions, as such, there is no quality that enables us to distinguish some of them as refering to an external world. "We may observe that it is neither upon account of the involutariness of certain impressions as is commonly supposed, nor of their superior force and violence that we attribute to them a reality as continued existence, which we refuse to others that are voluntary and feeble. For, our passions and affections—which we never suppose to have any existence beyond our perception—operate with greater violence and are equally involuntary as the impression of colour and sound which are supposed to be permanent things. The heat of a fire, when moderate, is supposed to exist in the fire, but the pain, which it causes on a nearer approach, is not taken to have any being except in the perception."

If now we examine the contents of the impressions to which we ascribe continued existence, we find that they are possessed of two characteristic viz, **(1) a peculiar constancy, (2) and, if they change, a peculiar coherence or regularity in their changes.** "These mountains and horses and trees which lie at present under my eyes have always appeared to me in the same order and when I lose sight of them and soon after, find them returned upon me without the least alteration." So also "when I return to my chamber, after an hour's absence, though I find not my fire in the same situation in which I left it, still I am accustomed in other instances to see a like alteration produced in a like time whether I am present or I am absent." But how does this constancy and coherence of certain impressions go about to produce so extraordinary an opinion as that of continued existence of body? The answer is found in a peculiar tendency of the imagination. "When we have been accustomed to observe a constancy in certain impressions and have found that the perception of sound of ocean, for instance, return upon us after an absence or annihilation with like manner and in a like order as its first appearance, we are not apt to regard these interrupted perceptions as different (which they really are) but on the contrary consider them as individually the same upon account of this resemblance ...". The two impressions are not identical but similar and, for this, we posit external object. Our imagination smoothly passes from one impression to the similar other, so as to think all of them as continuous.

"This resemblance is observed in a thousand instances and naturally connects together our ideas of these interrupted perceptions, by the strongest relation and conveys the mind with an easy transition from one to the other. An easy transition or passage of the imagination along the idea of different and interrupted perception is almost the same disposition of mind with that in which we consider one constant and uninterrupted perception. The thought moves along the successions with equal facility as if it is considered with only one object, and therefore confuse the succession with identity."

The same thing comes about from the side of coherence. "The imagination when set into a train of thinking is apt to continue even when its object fails it, and like a galley put in motion, carries on its course without any new impulse. Objects have a certain coherence even as they appear to our senses, but this coherence is much greater and more uniform if we suppose the objects to have a continued existence, and as mind is once in the train of observing an uniformity among objects, it naturally continues till it renders the uniformity as complete as possible."

"But though imagination has a strong tendency to perceive objects as identical and possessing a continued existence our reason may tell us otherwise. For if perception and objects be one, the actual interruption of our ideas will contradict the propensity for imagining them continuous. But the hypothesis of the **double existence of perception and objects** will solve these difficulties and will please our reason in allowing that dependent perceptions are interrupted and different and at the same time is agreeable to the imagination, in attributing a continued existence to something else which we call object. But this is only to lay one fiction upon another and fall back into the error which Berkeley had shown of distinguishing the objects as existent from the objects of perception."

Hume's conclusion regarding the existence of external objects as causes of our perceptions (impressions) is that **it is belief produced by our imagination.** "His point is that we have an inevitable and ineradicable propensity to believe in the continuous and independent existence of bodies" (Copleston, Vol. 5). It is a kind of blind faith, which not only the human beings, but also the animals entertain. We can prove the reality of external objects neither by reason; nor by experience. 'We cannot get outside the series of our perceptions to compare them with anything apart from them.'

VIII. Humean Conception of Self or Soul

Hume does not believe in a soul substance or a permanent self, which is the substratum of all our fleeting mental states. The explanation of the illusion of personal identity is the same as in the case of the material substance.

Some people claim that they have knowledge of 'soul' or self as an identical and permanent entity, and that they are immediately conscious of self. But as all our ideas are derived from the impressions, from what impression then could this idea of self be derived? It any impression gives rise to the idea of self that impression must remain invariably the same throughout our life, since self is believed to be something constant and abiding. But there is no such impression which is constant and invariable. It cannot be from any of these impressions that 'idea' of self is derived and consequently it is not a true idea. Self is a conscious, eternal entity, which we know by direct experience. But Hume says that all our ideas are derived from impression. From what impression do we get the idea of self or soul? [The self or soul being permanent or unchangeable, the impression from which it has been derived must be permanent or unchangeable, throughout our life. But such an impression is not available in experience. All our perceptions, all our impressions are always changing.] We have no impression of the idea of permanent self. The idea of Self is I enter most intimately into what I call myself. I always stumble on some particular perception or other, of heat or cold, light or shade, love or hatred, pain or pleasure. I never can catch myself at any time without a perception."

The explanation of the **illusion of personal identity** is the same as in the case of the material substance. In one case as in the other, a variable and interrupted existence is mistaken by the imagination for an uninterrupted and invariable existence, related objects are mistaken because related, for identical objects. "Our notion of personal identity proceeds from smooth and uninterrupted progress of thought along a train of connected ideas. In the case of external things it is very obvious. We do not cease to speak of a material thing as the same thing although a change has taken place within it; provided that change is small in comparison with the whole. ("The separation of a very small particle from any ordinary thing would not make us think of that as a different thing and) even a great change may take place in a thing without its being considered as a different substance, provided that change takes place gradually and imperceptibly. Even when the extent of change is eventually noticeable the illusion of identity will remain if only the new combination serves the same end, e.g. a ship altered by frequent repairs. In all these cases the transition from one idea to the other is so easy that they really appear to be the same."

Men may call themselves persons but in reality they are nothing but a bundle or collection of different perceptions which succeed each other with an inconceivable rapidity and are in a perpetual flux and movement. The mind is a kind of theatre where several perceptions successively make their appearances, glide away and mingle in an infinite variety of postures and situations. The comparison of theatre must not mislead us. They are the successive perceptions only that constitute the mind.

The question arises, then, how is this false idea of personal identity originated? What is the impression that gives us the idea of a person who remains unchanged thoughout all his changes? Hume says that, in fact, there is no such impression. But our imagination takes the similar but different impressions as identical. A child grows into an adult. His body has changed, his mind changes. Yet we believe that he is the same child. Why? Because the change is small and slow. If anybody sees him after a long time, say a few years, he recognises the great change the child has gone through. But those who perceive him everyday are unable to find it out. The change that occurs everyday in the child's mind and body is ignored and we see an identical person who remains unchanged in spite of all his changes. Our imagination helps us here—self or soul is nothing permanent, but is a bundle of impressions or mental states which are continuously bound together by the laws of association. The passage from one impression to another, here, is so easy that they seem to be the same.

Hume's fundamental mistake lies in thinking that self is a particular impression, but self is rather the principle of organisation of impressions. It is the very presupposition of impressions. Hume wanted to find this self from among the impressions where it could not be found.

But it may be noted that denial of self on the part of Hume was made quite late in the system of his philosophy. It would have been a very awkward situation for Hume if he had denied it earlier, for his doctrine of causality and his explanation of our belief in the external world tacitly assumes the existence of a permanent self. Causality, e.g. depends, for Hume, on association. Association presupposes memory and memory is impossible unless the past is retained and united with the present through the unity of the self.

Again, in explaining the belief in the external world Hume speakes of the "smooth progress of imagination along a series of impressions". But this is meaningless if there is no permanent self to exercise the imagination.

Besides, any mental process presupposes a substance 'mind', whose process it is. 'Perception without a perceiver' is inconceivable. Moreover, if the bundle of mental states is the 'self', then there is no distinction between one mind and other. How can we understand that this mental state belongs to this bundle? If Hume's view is accepted, there would have been no distinction between 'my' mind, and 'your' mind or 'his' mind.

When Hume says "when I enter......" etc. who is this "I"? It must be some substance behind and beyond the perceptions of love and hatred, pain or pleasure.

Lastly, we can say that memory becomes impossible without reference to a permanent self. This self is the precondition of all knowledge. It is the principle of unity among fleeting mental states. Immanuel Kant, the famous German philosopher who came after Hume, in the history of philosophy, criticised Hume from this standpoint. Self is an a priori principle of unity and is a precondition of all knowledge. It is always knower and never the known.

IX. Hume as a Sceptic

David Hume is the most consistent empiricist and carries out in his philosophy the sceptical consequences which logically follow from the findings of Locke and Berkeley. Exposed to Hume's criticism, the world of knowledge which Locke has so laboriously constructed disappears altogether and disintegrates into separate and disconnected elements among which there is no bond of union, no principle of organisation. Berkeley has criticised the material substance of Locke but, inconsistently to his empirical position, he has maintained spiritual substances to be real. Hume, in his turn, shows the unreality of the spiritual substance as well and reduces both the material and the spiritual world into a series of loose disconnected and discrete sensations. His criticism against the law of causality reduces it to simply a psychological habit of expectation due to custom. So now, there is no way to connect present with the past or future impressions.

So, given Locke's premises, there remains in the final conclusion nothing substantial, systematic, or necessary but merely the fleeting impressions of the moment. Philosophy of Hume is the last word of empiricism. Here reason is employed to show the weakness of reason and reason is turned against itself.

In the last chapter (XII) of his "Enquiry Concerning Human Understanding", Hume declares himself to be a sceptic. A sceptic denies the very possibility of knowledge. It is an enquiry into the conditions of knowledge. Hume defined his scepticism as mitigated or academical scepticism. His scepticism is a developed form of Pyrrho's uncompromising scepticism. Hume says that causal relation is only a product of imagination, a habit of expectation due to custom. There is no objective basis of this relation. It may be that, in the past, two events occured repeatedly one after the other, and we expected one with the appearance of the other. Yet there is no guarantee that in future also such correlation between two events will be observed. So all our inferences regarding future events are uncertain, probable and doubtful. All our knowledge regarding matters of fact is based on the relation of cause and effect. So, according to Hume, all our knowledge of matters of fact is uncertain and probable.

But though Hume is a sceptic regarding our knowledge of matters of fact, he admits our natural instinct towards the reality of external objects, even knowledge of matters of fact, as true. The water quenches our thirst or consuming poison results in death, fire burns, or dark cloud produces rain,—are true; because doubting them is not beneficial for our life. As B. Russell puts it, "If we believe that fire warms or water quenches, it is because it costs us too much pains to think otherwise. We cannot help believing, but no belief can be grounded in reason." Hume says that he enjoys everything of this world as a common man does, yet when he philosophises—he does not believe in everything but doubts in many well-accepted views.

This is why Morris observed that Hume 'was less a sceptic than he thought himself to be. He never applied his scepticism against natural sciences, history, geography, sociology, algebra, arithmetic, mathematics because the contradictory of this knowledge is not logically impossible. He was a sceptic in his views regarding 'false metaphysics'—which are discussions on super-natural, super-sensible objects like theology. As he himself observes: If we take in hands any volume of divinity or school of metaphysics . . . let us ask, "Does it contain any abstract reasoning concerning quality or number? No. Does it contain any experimental reasoning concerning matters of fact and existence?—No. Commit it then to the flames, for it can contain nothing but sophistry and illusion" (Enquiry).

Hume was a sceptic no doubt. But "his scepticism was," as Copleston observes, "a healthy antidote to dogmatism and fanaticism. Later philosophers in history or philosophy, like the Logical Positivists and Phenomenalists, are very much indebted to Hume's straightforward scientific attitude towards philosophy. Kant, the greatest philosopher of modern times, observed that it is Hume who woke him from his dogmatic slumber. Hume's scepticism is inescapable for an empiricist."

Immanuel Kant

(1724-1804)

9

CHAPTER

I. His Life and Works

Immanuel Kant was a German philosopher. He was born in Konigsburg in East Pruessia in 1724. He took admission in Konigsburg University in 1740 and studied different subjects like Physics, Mathematics, Geology, Astronomy, Philosophy etc. As a student he was extraordinarily brilliant. After finishing his studies here, he started teaching in this university as a professor in 1770. He taught mathematics, physics, pedagogy and philosophy. In 1781, at the age of 57, he wrote his world famous book, "Critique of Pure Reason". He is generally regarded as the greatest philosopher of modern times. Kant was a man of regular habits. People used to set their watches by him as he passed their doors. He spent his whole life in his birthplace Konigsburg. He was not an orthodox Christian, and preferred morality to religion. Kant died in 1804.

His famous writings are (1) The Critique of Pure Reason (1784), (2) The Critique of Practical Reason (1788), (3) The Critique of Judgment, (4) Fundamental Principles of the Metaphysics of Morals (1786), and many others.

II. Introduction to Kant's Philosophy

The two opposing trends of empiricism and rationalism had ultimately found a synthesis in Kant, who recognised the roles of both sensation and pure reason in knowledge. Both empiricists and rationalists made extravagant claims and, in the long run, fell into self-contradiction. If all our conceptions arise from sense perception, as the empiricists claim, then not only the science of the supersensible, but also the natural sciences would be impossible. The reason is simply this: we come to know particular cases alone through sense-experience. Sense perception never yields necessary and universal truth and without necessary and universal truth which are valid for every reasoning being, we are confined to the very narrow limits of singular cases. In Hume, the self-destructive nature of empiricism was evident in scepticism and probablism.

Rationalism went to an extreme in so far as it believed that it had discovered an "infallible criterion of truth in the clearness and distinctness of ideas and assure example for philosophical method, in the method of mathematics." This criterion of truth is not sufficient as is evident from the fact that the opposing philosophical systems of Leibniz and Spinoza were built on equally clear and distinct ideas.

Induction—which was recommended by Bacon as a substitute for the barren syllogistic method of the rationalists—has the advantage of increasing knowledge, but it leads us only to probables, not to strict universality, whereas the syllogism of the rationalists has the advantage of yielding universal and necessary truths, but it can only explicate and establish knowledge but cannot extend it as does induction.

The philosophy of Kant is meeting of the extremes, a historical crossroad of European thought. Here Rationalism and Empiricism meet together and are transformed. Kantian philosophy is neither empiricism nor rationalism, but it derives important truths from both these traditions. Kant digs beneath them both to find principles more fundamental than any perceived by these earlier schools. His new mode of thought is known as "philosophical criticism". Kant's criticism undertakes to sketch the limits of trustworthy human knowledge; and in this sense it may be said to continue, in a rigourous and very systematic way, an enterprise upon which Locke had already cautiously embarked. As B. Russell puts it: "To none of Kant's predecessors, 'knowledge' itself was a problem. But Kant brought the problem of knowledge to our notice in an easy but technical way. In fact Kant is supposed to have founded a new science viz, the science of knowledge, or Epistemology."

III. Everybody admits that 'knowledge' in the most indisputable sense is found in scientific knowledge. According to Kant, **two essential characteristics of scientific knowledge are (1) Universality, and (2) Newness.** The element of newness is derived from experience, no doubt, but the element of universality, which we find in pure physics, must be a priori, i.e. derived from some other source than experience.

Kant was very much influenced by his contemporary philosophers like Leibniz and Wolf. He supported rationalism in so far as it holds that reason alone can give us universal and necessary knowledge. Later, he was acquainted with British Empiricism, specially with the philosophy of David Hume. He was so much impressed with Hume's empiricism that he frankly admitted that "Hume first interrupted my dogmatic slumber and gave me an entirely new direction to my inquiries in the field of speculative Philosophy." And Kant started thinking that sense-experience gives us only appearance of the object to the mind. It is not possible for human mind to know the object as it really is.

Pre-Kantian thinkers used to believe that knowledge is either (i) self-evident, universal and necessary; or (ii) it is informative, but probable and uncertain. The rationalists before Kant believed that reason is the only source of knowledge. The empiricists believed that sense experience is the only source of knowledge.

Kant appreciated the rationalists when they said that reason gives us the universal and necessary element of knowledge. He appreciated Hume when he said knowledge is derived from sense-experience which, though uncertain, yet gives us new information.

Rationalists like Descartes, Spinoza, and Leibniz holds that all propositions are analytic. In an analytic proposition or judgment, the predicate **only analyses the subject-concept and adds nothing new.** The predicate is contained in the subject. For instance we may know that 'a triangle is a figure', or "a dog is an animal". Here the predicate only analyses what was already contained in the subject. The judgment thus is **self-evident** and **necessary**. It is true for all times, past, present, and future. So it is **universal** also. We need not take the help of sense-experience to prove that the judgments are true. Analytic propositions are thus **a priori**. Such judgments are based on the principle of non-contradiction. We should contradict ourselves, in the above examples, if we say that a dog is not an animal, or a triangle is not a figure.

The empiricists, on the other hand, hold that sense-experience is the only source of knowledge. So all knowledge is a posteriori, which means, knowledge comes after experience. All propositions are synthetic and a posteriori. In a synthetic judgment the predicate asserts or denies something that was not to be found in the subject. The predicate adds something new to the subject-concept. It is informative. The judgment 'some dogs are Spaniel' is a synthetic proposition. By examining the idea of dog we cannot trace any connection between dog and Spaniel. Yet we learn from experience that Spaniel is connected with dog. Such synthetic judgments are a posteriori or derived from experience. Such propositions are not universally and necessarily true. It is **experience** which shows whether the propositions are true or false. These are a **posteriori**, and only happens to be true, are contingently true. The denial of such synthetic 'a posteriori' judgments are **not self-contradictory**. We can easily think that 'some cats are not black', or 'some dogs are not Spaniel'.

According to the Rationalists only analytic a priori proposition is knowledge proper. According to the empiricists knowledge is synthetic a posteriori. **Kant discovered a third type of knowledge** which is expressed in **'synthetic a priori judgments.'** Such knowledge is universal and necessary as they are 'a priori', and, at the same time, adds something new to the concept of subject, as they are synthetic. **According to Kant, knowledge begins with experience, but all knowledge is not derived from experience**. Knowledge is a joint-product of both reason and experience. Reason gives universality and necessity, and experience gives newsness.

Kant is supposed to have founded a new science viz, the science of knowledge or epistemology. "To none of Kant's predecessors 'Knowledge' was a problem. But Kant brought the problem of knowledge to our notice, in an easy but technical way." Everybody admits that 'knowledge' in the most indisputable sense is found in scientific knowledge. Kant said that two essential characteristics of scientific knowledge are (1) Universality, and (2) Newness. Mathematics and pure physics are good examples of science. Kant compares Metaphysics with Mathematics and Physics and comes to the conclusion that while these two sciences are growing fast metaphysics shows no growth.

The main question that Kant asks in this context is: **How the natural sciences, which are based on experience, can give us universal and necessary knowledge**? His explanation is that these sciences arrived at the royal road of science through a **revolution in their way of thought, viz that the object of knowledge is not given ready-made in experience, but are constructed by the knower**. Kant claims that pure mathematics, geometry, pure physics give us knowledge that is universal and necessary, and at the same time adds some new information. By experience we can never arrive at a truly universal judgment, which is true at all times and places and for everybody. Such knowledge, if it exists, must be a priori, i.e. derived from **some source other than experience** or independent of experience. According to it anything to be known a priori, with certainty, for example in geometrical figures, can only be what follows necessarily from **what we ourselves have put into it** in drawing it according to our concept.

The purpose of Kant's most important book "The Critique of Pure Reason" is to prove that though none of our knowledge can transcend experience, it is nevertheless in part 'a priori'.

Kant's Conception of Synthetic a Priori Knowledge

Kant here separates two distinctions. On the one hand there is the distinction between **'analytic'** and **'synthetic'** propositions, on the other hand the distinction between **'a priori'** and **'a posteriori'** or empirical.

An analytic proposition is one in which the predicate is part of the subject, for instance, 'Black cats are black', or "a tall man is a man"—such propositions just analyse the subject term in the predicate. These propositions follow from the law of contradiction. To maintain that a tall man is not a man would be self-contradictory. A synthetic proposition is one that is not analytic. All the propositions that we know only through experience are **synthetic**. We cannot, by a mere analysis of concepts, discover such truths as, 'Tuesday was a wet day' or 'Alexander invaded India'. According to Kant, though all analytic propositions are analysis of the subject in the predicate, all synthetic propositions are known through experience.

An a posteriori or empirical proposition is one which we cannot know without the help of sense-perception. Whenever our knowledge of the truth of a proposition depends on observational data,—it is a posteriori or empirical. **An a priori proposition**, on the other hand, is one which, though derived from experience, is seen, when known, to have a basis other than experience. A child, when learning arithmetic, may take the help of four marbles to know that two and two make four. But when he has grasped that 'two and two make four' he no longer requires confirmation by instances. 'The proposition has a certainty which induction can never give to a general law.' All the propositions of pure mathematics are in this sense 'a priori. Universality and necessity are the two characteristics of 'a priori' propositions, whereas, addition of some new information is the characteristic of 'empirical' or a posteriori propositions.

Hume proved that the law of causality is not analytic but synthetic, the truth of a causal proposition is not absolute. Kant accepted Hume's view that it is **synthetic**, but nevertheless maintained that it is known **a priori**. According to him, arithmetic and geometry also are **synthetic** but are, likewise, **a priori**. Kant claimed that neither analytic a priori propositions, nor synthetic a posteriori propositions are knowledge proper, but it is **synthetic a priori propositions only** that yield scientific knowledge.

So Kant was led to formulate his problem in these terms:

How synthetic judgments a priori are possible?

According to Kant all **judgments of mathematics are synthetic a priori**, e.g. 7 + 5 = 12, this mathematical proposition is universally and necessarily true. So it is not derived from experience, but is a priori. It is derived from our reason. Again, the proposition is synthetic, because the concept of 12 is not contained in 7 + 5, it is something new. Thus, according to Kant, the proposition 7 + 5 = 12 is a priori and synthetic.

Pure Geometry also gives us synthetic a priori propositions, e.g., "The straight line between two points is the shortest." It is synthetic because the concept of 'straight' contains no notion of quantity, but only of quality. The concept of the 'shortest' is wholly an addition and it cannot be derived from any analysis of the concept of a straight line. The proposition is also a priori because it is universal and necessary. Universality and necessity cannot be derived from experience.

In **Pure Physics** too, there are synthetic a priori propositions. "Every event must have a cause", this fundamental principle of pure physics is 'synthetic a priori'. It is **a priori** because it states universal and necessary truth. It is not derived from experience. Kant thinks that Hume was wrong when he thought that our knowledge of causal principle is derived from experience. The principle also means that it cannot be otherwise. We may not know the cause, but the cause must be there—the judgment "Every event must have a cause" is **synthetic** because the idea of 'cause' is not contained in the concept of 'event'. An event is that which occurs, but it does not point beyond itself towards its cause, which is another event.

Thus scientific knowledge, though empirically derived, are a priori synthetic. Kant fully succeeds in showing how synthetic a priori judgments are possible in Mathematics, Geometry, and Pure Physics.

IV. Now his problem is to show **whether such knowledge is possible in metaphysics** or **whether synthetic a priori knowledge is possible in metaphysics also.** The last question arising out of the general problem is whether **metaphysics as a science of the super-sensible is possible.**

Both pure mathematics and pure science give us synthetic a priori propositions. They are based on experience, yet yields necessary and universals truths. Everybody admits that these are established scientific knowledge. But metaphysics does not exist as an established science. Since all attempts to answer metaphysical questions, such as whether the world has a beginning or is there from eternity, whether God exists or not, whether our soul is immortal—have always met with contradictions. Our reason cannot rest satisfied unless we can determine whether it is possible for us to know anything in the metaphysical field.

Now, if by scientific knowledge we mean synthetic a priori judgments only, then metaphysics—which deals with supersensible entities like God, soul etc.—are not "knowledge" in the Kantian sense of the term. All metaphysical propositions, though they try to give us synthetic a priori judgments, are based on our reason and intellect to the exclusion of experience altogether. These propositions cannot be verified by sense-experience. These are only analytic a priori and, therefore, not knowledge in the true sense of the term, claims Kant. **Metaphysics is impossible as a science of the supersensible**.

But Kant admits at the same time that metaphysics, as a natural propensity of human mind, is possible. The theoretical knowledge is denied of the supersensible, but Kant admits that we may still have practical knowledge of it, as is needed by morality and religion.

V. Kant's Copernican Revolution

In the preface to the second edition of his Critique of Pure Reason, he compares himself to Copernicus and says that he has effected **a Copernican revolution** in philosophy. Kant claims that he has brought a "Copernican Revolution" in philosophy by his new conception of knowledge as synthetic a priori. Copernicus brought a revolution in the field of Astronomy. People before Copernicus thought than the sun and stars moved round the earth. But Copernicus introduced the hypothesis that the earth itself moved round the sun. People before Kant thought that our knowledge had to conform to its objects: Kant tried the hypothesis that the objects conformed to our ways of knowing. By this hypothesis he could explain how we could have 'a priori' knowledge of objects. So long as one supposed that knowledge conformed to or simply copied the objects, which were given readymade in our experience, one could not explain how any a priori knowledge was possible. But if the objects conformed to our ways of knowing, i.e., if they were determined by our faculty of knowledge, then, to the extent they were so determined, they might be known even prior to experience.

Mathematics, Physics and Geometry give us universal, necessary and new knowledge through **a revolution in their way of thinking.** The object of knowledge in these studies are also constructed and not given readymade. We have first constructed a triangle making its three sides equal, then from that construction it follows that the triangle is equiangular. Physics also does not observe material objects as they are given in experience. They introduced experiment. In experiment we control the whole situation whose laws we want to determine. Thus, "we compel Nature, to produce processes in which we are interested" and try to find out the conditions under which they occur. This is how synthetic judgments a priori are possible in Mathematics and Physics.

Kant's question is **"Can we raise metaphysics to the status of a science through a revolution in the mode of our thought?"** He claims that he has brought such a revolution. He compares his achievement to the revolution brought about by Copernicus in Astronomy. It is the aim of the Critique of Pure Reason to provide an adequate answer to this question. **The hypothesis of Copernicus shows that our knowledge of objects depends on our position in space. Kant's hypothesis tells us that we do not know objects 'as they are' but as they** are **constructed** by our mind.

Kant concludes that we can never know the object as it is. Our mind does not passively receive the sense-manifold. It actively organises this material into an object of knowledge. Whenever we know anything, we apply certain a priori conditions (categories and forms) on the sense-content. Otherwise our sense-experience remains discrete and unorganised. Thus our mind constructs the object of knowledge.

Consequently **we know only the appearance of the object**, never the objects-in-themselves. Like a man who always wears a pair of blue spectacles sees everything always tinged with blue colour, and never the objects in their true colours, so the knower always knows the things as they appear through our a priori forms and categories, never the things-in-themselves. Our world of knowledge is thus an appearance, not reality, which always remains beyond the limits of human knowledge.

Metaphysics claims to give us **knowledge of reality, knowledge of super-sensible entities,** like God, soul, etc. which are never objects of any possible experience. Kant shows that such knowledge is not possible. Objects must first be presented to our sensibility. Mind actively constructs the object of knowledge by the forms (space and time) of sensibility and categories (substance, causality etc.) of the understanding. These (metaphysical) objects do not fulfil the fundamental conditions of human knowledge. As Falkenberg observes, **our intuitions (sense experience) without concepts (of the understanding) are blind and concepts without sense intuitions are empty**.

When we say that 'the flower is red' we must have the sense-intuition of a red flower. But mere sense-experience does not give us knowledge that "the flower is red". The sensations give us some impressions that are separate and independent of each other. It is not a meaningful whole. **In order to raise these discrete sense-content to the status of knowledge, we must apply the unifying principles of the understanding or categories like substance, and quality etc**. The red flower is a qualified substance. Red is the quality, flower is the substance. This is knowledge. The object of knowledge is thus a joint product of sensibility and understanding—Knowledge is synthetic a priori.

The world of objects or nature, though constructed by our understanding, is not a mirage or a dream. It is objectively real because each and every knower has to combine sensibility and understanding to construct the object of knowledge. **The forms and categories of heman mind are not the properties of any individual mind**. Rather, these are **universal and necessary pre-conditions of all knowledge**. Nature consists of objects of knowledge in so far as those are created by our understanding as a principle of unity. So Kant says that **understanding makes nature.**

Now, this world of knowledge is not the world of things-in-themselves which remain always unknown and unknowable, because, as soon as we know the thing-in-itself, it becomes an object of knowledge. It is no more the thing-in-itself or the unconditioned reality, but only thing—as it is known by our mind. This is **Kant's famous Copernican Revolution in Philosophy** which holds that in **knowledge, the object conforms to our ways of knowing, not that our ways of knowing conform to the object**.

According to Kant, the possibility of knowledge depends on a synthesis of sense experience and reason. Neither experience alone, nor reason alone can give us knowledge. **Our sense experience supplies us with the matter of knowledge, and reason, its form,** so that experience without reason is blind, and reason without experience is empty. The rationalists before Kant depended solely on reason and discarded experience altogether in their analysis of metaphysical problems like God, soul, freedom of the will etc. Such knowledge cannot be verified by experience. Knowledge for the rationalists was analytic a priori only. But such knowledge, though universal and necessary, are not synthetic a priori; so not 'knowledge' in the Kantian sense of the term.

Kant distinguishes between **appearance** and **reality**. Thing-in-itself is the reality. Appearances are objects of sensation. Appearances, when determined by the categories of the understanding, are called **Phenomena**. Things-in-themselves are called the **Noumena**, reality as thought not in terms of categories but as they are by themselves.

VI. Transcendental Aesthetic and Kant's Conception of Space and Time as a priori forms of intuition. By 'intuition' Kant means sensibility where the object is **given** directly. Whatever is given to our sensibility, must be given in Space and Time, i.e. it must be given in some place, at some time. According to Kant we have only sense-intuition. Intellectual intuition is not possible—Kant claims.

Kant is here undertaking a transcendental enquiry. Transcendental means for him an Epistemological enquiry in the a priori.

[The 'Critique of Pure Reason' consists mainly of three parts: Aesthetic, Analytic and Dialectic, dealing, respectively, with sensibility, understanding and Reason, showing, in the first two parts, how pure mathematics and pure science of nature are possible, and, in the last part, how metaphysics is impossible.]

Kant means by Transcendental Aesthetic the theory of sensibility in which he separates the a priori elements in our sensibility and points their significance for knowledge. These a priori forms are, according to Kant, Space and Time. These are also the a priori forms of all that can be given intuitively.

In transcendental exposition Kant says that the common man or the man in the street believes that space and time are two extra-mental receptacles in which objects exist and events occur. Realists like Locke etc. also take space and time to be real entities existing independently of the knowing mind. Kant rejects this commonsense view. According to him, **space and time are two forms of the knowing faculty of the human mind**. These belong to the sensibility or the capacity to receive representations when objects act upon us. Though they belong to the mind, **they are not subjective in the sense of being personal**. Space and time are **objective in the sense that these a priori forms of sensibility are universally and necessarity employed by the knowing mind on all objects and do not vary from individual to individual**. If anything is to be an object of knowledge it must be given in space and time. **Space and time are forms of sensibility**. They are the ways in which we intuit or perceive objects. We human beings are so constituted that we can perceive objects only spatially and temporally.

All sensed contents are ordered by the forms of space and time. These exist in mind a priori as mere forms of sensibility.

(a) **In metaphysical exposition, or metaphysical explanation of space and time** Kant shows, first, that space and time are not derived from experience but are **a priori** and secondly, that they are **intuitions** and **not concepts**. Here space and time are treated separately as far as possible.

(i) The first argument says that outer experiences are experiences of things in **space**. The idea of space makes these experiences possible. So it is not derived from experience.

(ii) The second argument says that idea of **space** is a priori, because it is a necessary idea and necessity is the mark of the 'a priori'. We may imagine the absence of all things in space, but we cannot imagine the absence of space itself. The first argument is negative in the sense it only shows that space is not empirically derived. The second argument positively says that it is **a priori**.

(iii) In **the third argument** Kant distinguishes between a general concept and a pure intuition and says that **space is not a general concept but is pure intuition**. Whenever we speak of space, we think that it is one, and particular spaces are its different parts. The mode of knowledge that relates itself directly to a single individual is intuition, not concept. The one single concept of space is not constructed out of the particular spaces. Here the whole precedes the parts, but in cases of concepts we start from the parts to the whole. So space is an **intuition** and **not a concept**.

(iv) **The fourth argument** establishes the same point that space is an intuition, not a general concept. A general idea like the idea of 'man' is equally present in each and every individual man. But space, having infinite magnitude, cannot be equally present in each thing of different magnitudes. So space is **not a general concept but an intuition**.

Moreover, a general concept has an infinite number of instances under it, but they are not contained within it. Particular men are instances of the general concept 'man', never a part of the general concept 'man'. But particular spaces are mere parts of one space. So space is not a general concept but must be an intuition.

(b) By **Transcendental exposition** Kant understands the "explanation of a concept as a principle from which the possibility of other a priori synthetic knowledge can be understood."*

Here Kant's argument is—**It is only on this view of space as an a priori intuition that the a priori synthetic character of geometrical knowledge is possible**. Geometrical propositions are necessary propositions. We know that three angles of a triangle is equal to two right angles. This knowledge is true not only of my present experience, but also of my past and future experiences. This necessity and universality is inherent in 'space' as **a priori** form of our sensibility. Geometry gives us synthetic knowledge, because space is not a concept but an **intuition** (as is shown in 3rd and 4th argument in metaphysical exposition).

*Kant's Critique of Pure Reason, Rashbehari Das

Metaphysical Exposition of Time

Kant put forward similar arguments to show that time is an a priori form of intuition, as he showed in his metaphysical and transcendental exposition of space. The first two arguments prove that time is a priori, the other two arguments prove that time is not a concept, but an intuition—

(i) **Firstly** time, according to Kant, is not an empirical concept derived from our experience of succession and co-existence of things rather our experiences of succession and co-existence presupposes the concept of time. Our idea of time precedes such experiences of co-existence and succession of events. So it is a priori.

(ii) **Secondly** we may think that no appearances are there in time, that time is empty. But we cannot think that time itself is not there. It is the universal precondition of all appearances. It is necessary and universal, therefore a priori.

(iii) **Third** argument shows that time is not a general idea or concept, but an intuition. There is only one time and hours seconds, minutes, etc. are parts of that one time. The experience of the whole precedes those of parts. The mode of knowledge here is, thus, intuition. We can recognise hours, minutes and seconds as parts of parts of time, only because the notion of time is there in our minds as form of intuition.

(iv) The **fourth** argument shows that time is not a concept or general idea but an intuition. What we call hours, minutes etc. are nothing but parts of one infinite time. Now, an idea or a concept of particular individual men are instances of that idea of 'man' which wholly or entirely exists in them. But Infinite and one time cannot wholly belong to particular parts of time. So time is an intuition, not a concept. It precedes our experience of time, and does not follow them. "In conception parts precede the whole, but in intuition the whole precedes the parts."

Transcendental Exposition of time explains the fact that it is on the basis of this nature of time, which is showed in the *metaphysical exposition* of time, i.e. time is a synthetic a priori form of the knowing mind that mathematics can offer us **synthetic a priori** judgments. The proposition "time has only one dimension" is synthetic a priori. This proposition is an axiom, such axioms lie at the basis of many other sciences like mechanics etc. and we know such propositions with absolute certainty. So it is a priori. The presence and absence of the same thing in one and the same place is understood only by the fact that they occur one after another, i.e. in time. This is why **mechanics** as a science gives us synthetic a priori judgments.

(v) **Space and time are not independent entities**. They are only subjective conditions of all our intuitions, says Kant. Space and time do not quality things-in-themselves. We know things in-themselves only under these two forms of intuitions. Newton took space to be independent reality and absolute entity. It is the objective view of space, and makes, as Kant comments, it absolutely real, eternal and infinite non-entity. Space and time are, according to Kant, two conditions of all our empirical knowledge.

Space, according to Kant, **is the form of all outer experiences**. That the object is out there in space is a knowledge that is possible only because space is the subjective condition of all our outer experiences.

Time is the form of **both outer and inner experiences**, because, according to Kant, even outer experiences belong ultimately to inner experiences as mind is the knower. All our experiences come in time, i.e. successively, one after another, not simultaneously.

"Lastly, Kant observes that **Space and Time are empirically real but transcendentally ideal**. They are empirically **real**, because no experience, outer or inner, is possible without these forms. They are transcendentally **ideal** because, from the point of view of Thing-in-itself, these are only properties of human mind. Space and time do not determine the thing-in-itself, they determine only its appearance. What the object of knowledge, apart from all relation to knowledge is, we do not and cannot know. Anything, if it is to be an object of knowledge, must be in some place, and at some time. Things-in-themselves are, therefore, never objects of knowledge, they remain always beyond our knowledge, they are unknown and unknowable."*

That space and time are empirically real, but transcendentally ideal, has been explained by Joad with a simple example. According to him, if we always wear a blue glass spectacles in our eyes, then we see everything as tinged with the blue colour. If it so happens that we are unable to see without wearing those spectacles, then it would not be possible for us to know the actual colour of the objects before us. They will always look bluish. The real colour of the object will always go beyond our knowledge. Space and time are like those coloured spectacles without which it is not possible for us to reach real objects of knowledge, or the things-in-themselves. We'll have to know things as they appear through these two forms of sensibility, space and time. Thus the things-in-themselves remain always beyond our knowledge.

Yet this world of known objects is not a mirage, or a dream, or anything unreal. Our world is a world of things-in-themselves as determined by our ways of knowing. The world that we know with space and time is **universal** and **necessary**. So this phenomenal world is not unreal. It appears same to all knowers. It is not subjective, the snake is a but is objective. Compare Kant's view with **Leibniz's view of space**. Leibniz considered space as unreal. Space is **confused perception** of monads. If our confused perception (sensation) becomes clear, space vanishes. It is illusion, reality is consciousness, monads are the only realities. This subjective view of space has been rejected by Kant.

Kant had distinguished between phenomena and noumena, between objects as they are known and objects as they are by themselves, between appearance and reality. But this distinction is not intelligible, because these are relative terms. Appearance is always the appearance of reality, and reality is that which appears to be such and such. Reality expresses itself through appearance, and, if appearance is known, reality cannot remain unknown and unknowable.

VII. Kant's Reconciliation between Opposed Views

(a) **Kant reconciled the opposed systems of Rationalism and the Empiricism.** The rationalists like Descartes, Spinoza and Leibniz took reason to be the sole source

*R. Das: Kant's Critique of Pure Reason

of knowledge and discarded experience altogether because, according to the rationalists, knowledge is universal and necessary. Experience gives us only probable knowledge, not certainty. Such knowledge varies from individual to individual. On the other, hand the empiricists like Locke, Berkeley and Hume were tired of reason and rational theories of Descartes, Spinoza and Leibniz. They discussed metaphysical problems, without any criticism of our knowing faculty, without ever asking the most fundamental question: 'How far our reason is capable of knowing reality?' So the empiricists rejected reason and tried to establish philosophical systems on the basis of experience only. But empirical knowledge is not necessary and universal, though it adds new facts about the object, our knowledge. So empiricists gave knowledge novelty at the cost of universality and necessity.

(b) Kant reconciled these two attitudes towards philosophy. He showed that reason and experience are both necessary for knowledge. Reason gives us universal and necessary element of knowledge, its form; and experience gives newness, the 'matter' of knowledge—knowledge, according to him, is both universal, necessary and it increases our existing stock of knowledge—Knowledge is a joint product of reason and experience. Our mind does not receive sensations passively, as the empiricists believed, rather, it actively constructs the object of knowledge out of the sense-manifold. Thus knowledge is both synthetic and a priori.

(c) Kant also **reconciles idealism with realism**. Idealists say that the world of knowledge, is a construction of mind—human or divine, whatever we perceive have no existence without reference to some mind or other. The world is ideal in nature, has no reality of its own. The realist, on the other hand, believes that the object of knowledge has an independent existence of its own. It exists, whether any mind knows it or not—Kant reconciled idealism and realism by positing the things-in-themselves. Things-in-themselves affect us somehow, our mind applies some a priori forms of space and time and categories of the understanding, on these affections or sense-manifold, unifies them and constructs the object of knowledge. This object, though not the things-in-themselves, is **not a dream**, or **mirage**. It is **'nature'**, as we know. It is not possible to know the objects without these preconditions supplied by the knower. Thus, for Kant, the objects of knowledge are both ideal and real, constructed by the knowing mind, as well as having some objective background in things-in-themselves. His theory is known as **Phenomenalism**. The realm of human knowledge is phenomenon, his theory is known as "Phenomenalism".

VIII. Importance of 'Things-in-Themselves' in Kant's Philosophy

'Things-in-themselves' occupy an important position in Kant's philosophy. It saves his theory from being subjective idealism, as we find in Berkeley. Kant's phenomena have their real origin in things-in-themselves, or the Noumena. The world of knowledge is not only the world of ideas, of finite minds or of God's mind.

It also saves his theory from the Realism of Locke. Locke's theory of knowledge is known in history of philosophy as **Representative Realism**. He admits the reality of both mind substance and the material substance. But both mind and matter substances are unknown and unknowable, because, mind is confined within the range of its ideas only. Ideas are copies of the objects, knowledge consists in right joining and separating of ideas. But truth consists in correspondence of ideas with reality. Mind passively receives ideas and only finds out connections among them. Thus it is not possible to know whether any idea or their combination corresponds to reality or not.

Kant avoids this defect of representative realism by admitting that mind is active in knowledge situation, and applies its a priori forms and categories on the sense-manifold, to make it knowledge proper. Kant distinguishes between objects as we know them (Phenomena) and objects as they really are. According to Kant, things-in-themselves always remains unknown and unknowable. This does not hamper our knowledge, because objects of knowledge are constructed on the basis of things-in-themselves (Noumena) by the knowing mind with the help of the pre-conditions of all knowledge and these pre-conditions—space, time, substance, causality etc.—are universal and necessary for all knowledge.

Kant is both a rationalist and an empiricist, both an idealist and a realist. He is a **rationalist** in so far as he admits the mind as an active principle, he is an **empiricist** in so far as he admits that experience is essential for knowledge. He is an **idealist** in the sense that, according to him, our mind constructs the object of knowledge. His famous saying is "understanding makes nature". He is a **realist** in the sense that things-in-themselves are there, behind and beyond our world of knowledge.

But things-in-themselves are unknown and unknowable. Kant is not a sceptic like Hume, who denies the very possibility of knowledge. Rather, he is an **Agnostic**, who admits the possibility of knowledge, but for whom reality is beyond our knowledge. Object as it is known and object as it is in itself—are not the same for Kant.

This dualism between the phenomena and noumena, the appearance and reality, the known world and the reality, has been criticised by later philosophers and commentators. 'Knowledge', which is not knowledge of the reality, is not 'knowledge' at all. Besides, the appearance is the appearance of reality, so that when we know the appearance, reality is not entirely unknown.

In fact, as Copleston remarks, "In asserting the existence of noumenon as the 'cause' of sensation Kant contradicts himself, that is to say, he is inconsistent with his own principles". Kant himself is applying the category of 'causality', 'existence' on the things-in-themselves, when he says that things-in-themselves exist, and are causes of our sense-intuitions.

Again, Kant said that the forms and categories of the knowing mind are universal and necessary for all knowledge, but these are properties of the knowing mind only, and not of the things-in-themselves. Hegel, the German philosopher, said later that the forms and categories of the knowing mind are also the properties of the things-in-themselves. Thus the fundamental dualism of Kant's philosophy was removed by Hegel.

IX. Transcendental Deduction of the Categories

Here Kant is proving the objective validity of the categories of the understanding. These are twelve in number, which he deduced from the faculty of judgment or thought, e.g. substance, causality, existence, unity. These categories underlie our experience.

Deduction means nothing but the demonstration of the objective validity of the categories. **Transcendental deduction** shows how the a priori categories, which are not derived from experience, are still valid of the objects of experience.

In the case of space and time, which are the a priori forms of sensibility, no transcendental deduction was necessary because, if any object is to be given to our sensibility, it can be given only in space and time. But the categories belong to the understanding and yet claim to determine all objects of knowledge, even metaphysical entities like God and Self, in so far as we think these as substances and causes. These concepts do not depend on experience. Therefore the question arises as to how far they are valid of objects.

Kant shows that the categories are the most general concepts of object, and without them no object can be thought. So, for the knowledge of objects given through sense and thought, the categories "must be recognised as 'a priori' conditions of the possibility of experience."

Knowledge is essentially a whole, or a unity. Sense-intuition is receptive, yet the sense-maxi-fold implies a synthesis of space and time by the mind. This receptivity of intuition is combined with the spontaneous activity of the understanding to yield knowledge. Mind or self, in its three-fold synthetic activity, gives rise to knowledge.

The self, for Kant, is, thus, not a substance but a principle of unity, which remains unknown and unknowable. Self-consciousness relates isolated sensations with each other and thereby converts them into cognisible objects forming parts of a single system which we call nature. **The co-relative of nature therefore as an orderly whole of parts necessarily related to each other, is mind. This is what Kant means by saying "understanding makes nature."** The manifold of sensation must be combined (otherwise they would not be known at all) and the categories are the modes of combination. This means that the categories, though subjective, yet have objective validity. [It must be remembered that, according to Kant, categories have application only within the realm of our experience. Whether they are applicable also in the realm of things-in-themselves or not—we do not know.]

X. The Ideas of Reason

Reason is conceived as distinct from the understanding. Reason is called the faculty of principles, whereas the understanding is faculty of rules.

We have seen that, according to Kant, categories cannot be used beyond experience. These are applied with confidence only when presentations are given to us in the forms of space and time. In other words, the categories have reference only to a sensible content, or to that which is received by us in the form of sensation. When Kant says that **'the understanding makes nature'** he is thinking of nature in the sense of an ordered system of our experience. He is quite well aware that there might be another nature outside our experience, which exists independently of sensible forms of space and time. But he does not prefer to make understanding responsible for an objective nature of this kind. The phrase "understanding makes nature" means, simply, that order is introduced into our experience through working of the categories.

Everything which enters into nature, as we know it, must come under the rule of the categories or of the conception of understanding.

Our experience, however, is not complete in itself. It points beyond itself to an objective source, i.e. to the noumenal world or the world of things-in-themselves. Of this objective world we can know nothing and, therefore, it does not come within the scope of our experience. The categories cannot be applied to it. We know its objects only as the unknown causes of our sensations. We know that this world of real things exist, but to attempt to gain a definite knowledge of it is futile. Nevertheless, we fall into a kind of transcendental illusion and attempt to **apply the categories to things of which we have no sensible experience.** We attempt to complete our knowledge as if it were actually possible for us to reach ultimate reality. We then construct a system of knowledge which has no validity but which are useful as **regulative ideas** pointing out that our so-called complete systems of knowledge can never be complete. Such ideas can be graded together as the **"Ideas of Reason"**. They are concerned with the (i) real nature of the soul, (ii) the world as a whole, (iii) and the ultimate Being or God. In making any statement about these entities, reason goes beyond experience and is attempting an impossible task. It becomes involved in illusion and, therefore, reaches its conclusions only by means of logical paralogism by contradiction or by unwarranted transition from thought to reality. The mistake lies in thinking that we have positive knowledge of objects corresponding to those conceptions. As a matter of fact, we have only negative knowledge, i.e. **ideas of reason** tell us that (a) our experience is not complete in itself. They (b) prevent us from being subjective idealists and thinking that there is no reality beyond our ideas.

The ideas of reason represent a **regulative ideal of the unity or completeness of our knowledge**. But this ideal always puts us beyond what we have already attained. The idea is an ineviable one, but it is one which we cannot realise. Kant examines these ideas and points out the flaws and inconsistencies which they reveal. God, Self or Soul, and the world as a whole, are the three ideas of reason. With equal force, we may argue that the world is limited in space and time and that it is unlimited, that God exists, and God does not exist, that the self or soul is a permanent substance, and it is not permanent—which show that the arguments, as Kant thinks, are logically sound yet they refute each other. This proves that we have entered a realm where we do not belong and where truth is not to be attained by logic.

The ideas are not pure illusions, "they are not merely arbitrary, they stand for an impulse which is ineradicable. The desire to grasp things as a whole is one which the reason can never forego but by science this aim is incapable of being attained. The value of the ideas can only be a **regulative value** within experience, not one that results in objective knowledge."

To sum up

Kant's **"Critique of Pure Reason"** consists of three main parts: Aesthetic, Analytic and Dialectic, dealing, respectively, with sensibility, understanding and reason. These are the three ways by which the 'knower' knows the objects. In short, he shows in the first two parts how pure mathematics and pure science of nature are possible, and, in the last part, how metaphysics is impossible.

Teranscendental Aesthetic: In Transcendental Aesthetic, Kant separates a priori elements in our sensibility viz. space and time and points out their significance in knowledge.

Kant distinguishes between things-in-themselves and things as they appear to our senses. 'Things as they are' affect us somehow. Our sensibility directly gets them, applies its forms Space and Time on them. In fact, these two are the a priori conditions of all knowledge. This means that whatever is presented before our sensibility must be given in some particular space and at some particular time.

Transcendental Analytic: This material of knowledge is then unified or synthesised by our understanding. The unifying principles or categories of the understanding are Substance, causality etc. These are twelve in number. When these are applied by the understanding on the sense manifold (which is already somewhat unified by the Forms of Sensibility) we get the object of knowledge. Object of our knowledge, therefore, is not given readymade to our sensibility and understanding. **The knower actively constructs it with its forms and categories.** Thus the objects of knowledge and the Things-in-Themselves are different. Things as they are, and things as we 'know' them are not the same. The knower actively participates in knowledge situation. By applying the forms and categories (a priori conditions of knowledge) the knower changes the character of Things-in-Themselves, so that, Things-in-Themselves are never known. These are, for Kant, unknown and unknowable.

Yet knowledge is important and useful, because the forms and categories which the knowing mind applies to the object of knowledge are not private and personal. These are universally applied in every case of knowledge. The knower must use these to know the object. Kant claims,—these forms and categories are the 'a priori conditions' of **all** knowledge.

Transcendental Dialetic: Metaphysics, which, deals with Thing or Reality-as-it-is, can never be a successful study. Knowledge, here, is impossible. The Ideas of Reason like God, Soul and the world as a whole, are obtained by applying the categories not on the sense-manifold but directly on Things-in-Themselves. We say '**God** exists', '**Soul** is immortal', etc. But these objects never appear in space and time. Knowledge requires both sense-experience and reason. God, self or soul, and the world as a whole—are, therefore, not objects of knowledge. These Ideas of Reason have only some regulative value. We realise, at this stage, that our knowledge can never extend beyond the field of possible experience.

MODEL QUESTIONS

PLATO

1. How does Plato show that knowledge is neither perception, nor opinion?
2. What is knowledge proper according to Plato? What are its different grades? Explain in this context Plato's 'Allegory of the Cave'.
3. Explain the doctrine of Ideas or Forms as formulated by Plato.
4. Show how the Ideas are related to one another. How are these related to particular things?
5. Critically consider Plato's doctrine of universals.
6. How does Plato conceive the Idea of the Good? What place does this idea occupy in his philosophical system?
7. Write short notes on:

   (a) Dialectic method of Socrates, (b) Universals, (c) Allegory of the Cave, (f) Idea of the Good.

ARISTOTLE

1. What is Form? What is matter? Explain with reference to Aristotle.
2. Discuss fully how Aristotle criticises Plato's doctrine of Forms or Ideas.
3. Explain and examine Aristotle's criticism of Plato's doctrine of Ideas (Forms).
4. Compare and contrast the views of Plato and Aristotle on the relation between universals and particulars.
5. Fully consider Aristotle's account of different kinds of causes with suitable examples.
6. Write short notes on:

   (a) Efficient cause, (b) Distinction between Form and Matter according to Aristotle.

DESCARTES

1. Enumerate the characteristics of modern philosophy and show that Descartes is rightly called the 'Father of Modern Philosophy.'
2. Explain fully Descartes' method of Philosophy. How does he arrive at his first principle with the help of this method?
3. What is 'cogito, ergo sum'? What are its different implications?
4. How does Descartes explain the existence of external world with the help of his first principle?
5. Criticially consider Descartes' theory of Ideas, with special reference to his doctrine of Innate Ideas.
6. Analyse fully Descartes' proofs for the existence of God, and comment on them.

7. Discuss the 'Criterion of Truth' as propounded by Descartes. Is he consistent with his criterion?
8. What is a Substance for Descartes? Do you agree with his view? Critically comment.
9. Write short notes on:

   (a) Interactionisms, (b) Cogito, ergo sum, (c) Ontological proof for the existence of God, (d) Innate Ideas according to Descartes.

SPINOZA

1. Explain clearly Spinoza's doctrine of Substance with reference to his dictum 'Determination negatio est'.
2. What is an Attribute? How are Spinoza's Attributes related to Substance? Is he consistent in his view?
3. Elucidate "Substance = God = Nature" and criticise Spinoza's Monism.
4. How does Spinoza define Modes? What, in Spinoza's view, is the relation between Substances and Modes? Do the Modes have only subjective or real being?
5. Explain how mind and body are related according to Spinoza. Explain in this context his theory of psycho-physical parallelism.
6. Analyse Spinoza's theory of knowledge, with special reference to his theory of various grades of knowledge.
7. Write short notes on:

   (a) Infinite modes, (b) Freedom of will in Spinoza's philosophy, (c) Spinoza's method, (d) Relation of One and many in Spinoza's philosophy.

LEIBNIZ

1. What is a substance for Leibniz? How does his definition differ from that of Descartes and Spinoza? Is he successful in explaining the relation of God and the world, one and many?
2. Fully consider Leibniz's Theory of Monads. How can there be a system of monads if 'monad's are 'windowless'?
3. Critically consider Leibniz's explanation of Mind-Body relation and compare his view with those of Descartes and Spinoza.
4. Give a brief account of Leibniz's theory of knowledge and compare it with that of Descartes and Locke.
5. Critically consider the views:

   (a) All ideas are innate

   (b) Some ideas are innate, and

   (c) No ideas are innate.

6. Write short notes on:

   (a) Pre-established harmony, (b) Identity of indiscerables, (c) Law of Sufficient Reason, (d) Leibniz's Law of Continuity, (e) Perception and apperception in monads, (f) All ideas are innate.

LOCKE

1. What are Innate Ideas? How does Locke refute the doctrine of Innate Ideas? Show how far Locke's criticism applies to Descartes' theory of Innate Ideas.
2. Explain clearly Locke's theory of the origin of knowledge with special reference to his classification of Ideas.
3. What is knowledge according to Locke? Discuss how far Locke is consistent in developing his theory of the degrees of knowledge.
4. How does Locke distinguish between primary and secondary qualities of Matter? How far is this distinction tenable?
5. Give a critical exposition of Locke's theory of knowledge with special reference to his theory of substance.
6. Write short notes on:

   (a) Locke's conception of mind as a 'tabula rasa', (b) 'Substance is that we know not what', (c) Locke's conception of Innate Ideas, and their criticism, (d) Influence of Descartes on Locke.

BERKELEY

1. How does Berkeley refute Locke's Representation Realism? Explain fully and comment critically on Berkeley's view.
2. What are abstract general Ideas? How does Berkeley refute them and why?
3. What are Berkeley's arguments against the distinction between primary and secondary qualities?
4. Critically consider how Berkeley attacks Locke's definition of Substance.
5. Explain Berkeley's 'Esse-est-percipi' and show how explanation external material world leads to the Scepticism of Hume?
6. What is Idealism? What is Subjective Idealism? Is Berkeley's Idealism Subjective or Objective?
7. Write short notes on:

   (a) "Esse est percipi", (b) Solipcism, Subjective Idealism, and Objective Idealism, (c) Rejection of the distinction between Primary and Secondary qualities, (d) Development of British Empiricism from Locke to Hume.

HUME

1. Distinguish between "Relations of Ideas" and "Matters of Fact" as explained by Hume. How do we know matters of fact, according to Hume?

2. How does Hume distinguish between Impressions and Ideas? Explain the importance of this distinction in Hume's philosophy and examine.
3. Fully consider Hume's doctrine of Self along with his explanation of personal Identity.
4. What is a Substance? How does Hume reject the notion of a permanent Substance and why?
5. Explain, after Hume, the relation between cause and effect. Has the cause any power to produce the effect? Discuss fully.
6. How does Hume explain the continued and independent existence of the external world? How does he explain personal identity?
7. What is Scepticism? Is Hume a Sceptic? Why is Hume called an Academic Sceptic?
8. Write short notes on:
   (a) Necessity in causal relation, (b) "Logical consequence of Locke's Empiricism is Hume's Scepticism"—Explain, (c) Importance of his view regarding causal relation on his whole philosophy.

KANT

1. What is Kant's problem? How does he solve it?
2. What do you understand by Kant's Copernican Revolution? What does it imply?
3. Explain, in short, how, according to Kant, Mathematics is possible, how physical sciences are possible, but metaphysics as a science is not possible?
4. Distinguish between synthetic and analytic propositions. How are these related to a posteriori and a priori propositions? Are synthetic a priori propositions possible? Discuss with reference to Kant.
5. Write short notes on:
   (a) 'Intuition' as Kant understood it, (b) Kant's Copernican Revolution, (c) Understanding makes Nature.

CALCUTTA UNIVERSITY QUESTION PAPERS

PHILOSOPHY HONOURS

Second Paper 2006

(New Syllabus)

Full Marks 100

The figures in the margin indicate full marks. Question No. 1 is compulsory. Answer **any five** from the rest:

1. Answer in brief (**any five**): 5 × 4

(a) Are knowledge and belief different from each other according to Plato? (b) How many types of causes are recognised by Aristotle? Mention their names and give examples. (c) What is the main texts of Interactionism as a theory of the relation between mind and body? (d) What are the different stages of knowledge according to Spinoza? (e) What is the Law of Sufficient Reason as stated by Leibniz? (f) How does Locke distinguish between primary and secondary qualities? (g) How many types of complex Ideas are accepted by Locke? Give examples of each type. (h) Mention only one argument by Berkeley for refuting the abstract general idea. (i) Which propositions are admitted by Hume as expressions of Relations of Ideas? (j) How does Kant distinguish between a priori and a posteriori knowledge?

2. What is the characteristic of knowledge proper according to Plato? How does Plato establish the theory that sense-perception is not knowledge proper? 6 + 10

3. How does Aristotle distinguish Matter from Form? Does he recognise the possibility of 'Pure Matter'? 12+4

4. How does Descartes arrive at his principle "Cogito, ergo sum"? Why is the principle regarded as the foundation of his philosophy? 8 + 8

5. Crities say that Spinoza upheld the 'One' at the expense of the 'Many'. Describe Spinoza's theory of the relation between God and the world and explain the relevance of such a critique. 10 + 6

6. Describe the characteristics of Monads according to Leibniz. If the Monads are windowless, how is the relationship among them established? 12 + 4

7. How does Locke refute the theory of Innate Ideas? What is the influence of this refutation on his theory of knowledge? 12 + 4

8. Is Berkeley a Solipcist? Discuss in detail. 16

9. How does Hume distinguish between Impressions and Ideas? What are the objections against this theory? 12 + 4

10. Explain and evaluate Hume's doctrine of Self. 12 + 4

11. Which judgments are a priori according to Kant? What is the difference between a priori analytic and a priori synthetic judgments? Discuss, following Kant, how synthetic a priori judgments are possible. 4 + 4 + 8

PHILOSOPHY HONOURS
Second Paper 2007
(New Syllabus)
Full Marks 100

Question No. 1 is compulsory. Answer **any five** from the rest:

1. Answer in brief (**any five**): 4 × 5

(a) What is the characteristic of knowledge proper, according to Plato? (b) Does Aristotle recognise the philosophy of 'Pure Matter'? (c) What does Descartes mean by "Criterion of Truth?" (d) Who expresses the "Intellectual Love of God" and how? (e) What is the nature of Substance according to Locke? (f) What is the main thesis of Berkeley's Idealism? (g) What does Hume mean by 'Impressions'? (h) What does Kant mean by Categories of Understanding?

2. Explain Plato's theory of Ideas. What are the important objections against this theory? 10 + 6

3. How many causes are accepted by Aristotle? Discuss how Aristotle criticises his predecessors while discussing the theory of causality. 12 + 4

4. Explain the concept of Substance as developed by Descartes, Spinoza and Leibniz. Is this Rationalist Theory of Substance acceptable? 12 + 4

5. What are the three kinds of knowledge admitted by Spinoza? Explain those with appropriate examples. 4 + 12

6. What is the Law of "Sufficient Reason" as accepted by Leibniz? If everything has sufficient reason for its existence, then how can one explain the contingent truths of experience? Discuss, after Leibniz. 10 + 6

7. How does Locke distinguish between the primary qualities and secondary qualities of Substance? Is this theory acceptable? 10 + 6

8. What is 'Abstract Idea'? Does Berkeley accept the existence of Abstract Idea? 4 + 12

9. Show the difference between Relations of Ideas and Matters of Fact, as explained by Hume. What is the basis of our knowledge regarding the Matters of Facts, according to Hume? 10 + 6

10. Give an account of the following two in the light of Kant's philosophy:

(a) Space and Time, (b) Copernican Revolution in the field of Knowledge. 8 + 8

11. Write explanatory notes on **any two:**

(a) Descartes argument for the existence of God, (b) Innate Idea, (c) God in Berkeley's Philosophy, (d) Hume's Scepticism. 8 + 8

PHILOSOPHY HONOURS

Third Paper 2008
(New Syllabus)
Full Marks 100
(Under 1 + 1 + 1 System—Part II)

Question No. 1 is compulsory. Answer **any five** from the rest:

1. Answer in brief (**any four**): 5 × 4

(a) What is the Cartesian "method of doubt"? (b) What, according to Spinoza, is an attribute? (c) What are the three kinds of knowledge admitted by Spinoza? (d) What is the Law of Sufficient Reason (Leibniz)? (e) What, according to Locke, are simple and complex ideas? (f) How does Locke distinguish between primary and secondary qualities? (g) Is Berkeley's Subjective Idealism solipsistic? Give reasons for your answer. (h) What are Berkeley's objections against Locke's distinction between primary and secondary qualities? (i) Is Hume Sceptic? Comment. (j) What, according to Kant, are the marks of a priori knowledge?

2. How does Descartes arrive at the principle "I think, therefore I am"? Is it an inferential truth? Discuss. 12 + 4

3. Explain and examine Descartes' causal argument for the existence of God. 8 + 8

4. Explain and examine Spinoza's theory of Substance. Does he uphold his theory of 'One' at the expense of Many? Give reasons for your answer. 12 + 4

5. What are 'Monads' according to Leibniz? If the monads are qualitatively different then how is the harmony of the universe maintained? 4 + 12

6. Explain Locke's objections to the doctrine of Innate Ideas. How does Locke account for the origin of knowledge? 10 + 6

7. How does Berkeley establish his theory of Subjective Idealism? What are the main objections against it? 10 + 6

8. How does Hume distinguish between Impressions and Ideas? What is the impact of this distrinction on his Theory of Causality?

9. (i) Distinguish, after Kant, between analytic and synthetic judgments.
   (ii) Are all a priori judgments analytic? Discuss. 8 + 8

10. How does Kant seek to show that space is an a priori intuition? 16

11. Write short notes on:

(a) Leibniz's distinction between truths of reason and truths of fact, (b) Hume's theory of self. 8 + 8

Part II
Third Paper 2009

Answer **Question No. 1** which is compulsory and **any five** from the rest:

1. Answer in brief (**any four**): 5 × 4

(a) Discuss any two objections of Locke against the theory of Innate Ideas.

(b) What is Representative Realism? (c) What does Berkeley mean by the statement "Esse-est-percipii'. (d) How does Hume distinguish between Impression and Idea? (e) How many types of ideas are accepted by Descartes? State with examples. (f) Why does Spinoza hold that substance is One and infinite? (g) What, according to Spinoza, is a 'mode'? (h) What is Pre-established Harmony according to Leibniz? (i) What, according to Leibniz, are the important characteristics of 'monads'? (j) Distinguish, after Kant, between analytic and synthetic judgments.

2. What is the criterion of truth according to Descartes? How does he arrive at this criterion? Discuss the importance of this criterion in Descartes' philosophy.

3. "Whatever is, is in God, and nothing can exist or be conceived without God." What does Spinoza mean by the statement? Explain after Spinoza, the relation between God and the world. 10 + 6

4. Explain the logical and philosophical significance of Leibniz's 'Law of Sufficient Reason'. 16

5. How does Locke distinguish between the primary and secondary qualities of Matter? How far is this distinction justified? 4 + 12

6. What is Abstract Idea? What is Berkeley's view on Abstract Ideas? Discuss. 4 + 12

7. Is Substance a self-subsistent entity? Compare the views of Substance as given by Descartes, Spinoza and Leibniz. 16

8. (a) How does Hume distinguish between propositions concerning relations of ideas and propositions concerning matters of fact?

(b) What, according to Hume, is the ground of our reasoning concerning 'matters of facts'? 4 + 12

9. (a) How does Kant seek to establish that space is not a concept but an intuition?

(b) "Space is a form of intuition".—Explain. 4 + 12

10. Write short notes on:

(a) Intellectual love of God in Spinoza's philosophy.

(b) Hume's scepticism. 4 + 12

Part II
Third Paper 2010
Full Marks 100

Answer **Question No. 1** and **any five** from the rest:

1. Answer in brief (**any four**): 5 × 4

(a) Explain, after Descartes, the Ontological proof for the existence of God. (b) What is the method of universal doubt? (c) What does Spinoza mean by the dictum, "Natura Naturata". Is it identical with "Natura Naturans"? (d) What, according to Leibniz, is the "Law of Sufficient Reason"? (e) Discuss the different degrees of knowledge admitted by Locke. (f) On what grounds does Berkeley reject the distinction between primary and secondary qualities? (g) Discuss Hume's view regarding causal necessity. (h) How does Kant distinguish between a priori and a posteriori judgments? (i) What, according to Spinoza, is an attribute? (j) What does the expression 'tabula rasa' mean? Who has used this term and in what context?

2. What is the first principle of Descartes' Philosophy? How does he arrive at it? Is it truly a first principle or a mere inferential truth? Discuss. 4 + 6 + 6

3. Explain and examine Spinoza's theory of Substance. Does he uphold the theory of 'One' at the expense of many? Give reasons for your answer. 12 + 4

4. Explain in brief Leibniz's doctrine of 'monads'. In what sense each 'monad' differ quantitatively and intrinsically from every other 'monad'? 10 + 6

5. What, according to Leibniz, is 'Pre-established harmony'? Can it adequately account for the relation of One and many? Discuss. 8 + 8

6. What are Innate Ideas? How does Locke refute the doctrine of Innate Ideas? 8 + 8

7. How does Locke define knowledge? How does he distinguish between intuitive, demonstrative, and sensitive knowledge? Is Locke's view regarding intuitive knowledge compatible with his general empirical outlook? 2 + 12 + 2

8. Give a critical account of Berkeley's thesis "Esse-est-percipii". 16

9. Explain how Descartes proved the existence of the external world. 16

10. Explain, after Hume, the distinction between impressions and ideas. What is the importance of this distinction in Hume's philosophy? Discuss. 10 + 6

11. What does Kant mean by "intuition"? How does Kant seek to establish that the idea of space is a priori? 10 + 6

Some exciting gifts are up for grabs with this book!!

A SHORT HISTORY OF WESTERN PHILOSOPHY

Dr Ira Sengupta

FREE Gifts Rs. 1000/-

Dear Readers

By now you must have gone through this book in the entirety. So we invite your assessment on this title with absolute impartiality and candid observations. After all, we publishers blindly depend on your benchmarking. Friends, please fill up the open spaces below with CAPITAL LETTERS. You may add some extra sheets of paper if the space provided is not sufficient for you.

i. What are the important topics of your syllabus which are not adequately covered in this book?

ii. In which chapters and on what topics the treatment of the subject-matter by the author is not satisfactory and why?

iii. Have you come across the typos, factual inaccuracies, inconsistencies, and other forms of mistakes in the book? If yes, then please specify the mistakes and page numbers.

iv. Name top three books on the same subject, which, in your consideration, are better than this book. Could you provide some reasons?

Your 1st Preference: ....

Your 2nd Preference: ....

Your 3rd Preference: ....

v. Any suggestion to improve the quality of illustrations, diagrams etc.?

vi. How did you like the cover design? Any suggestions on colours?

vii. Suggestions for further improvement of production standard:

viii. Who recommended you this book:

☐ Teacher ☐ Friend ☐ Parents ☐ Bookseller ☐ Librarian

ix. Name of the person who has recommended:

Designation: ....

Address: ....

Phone No.: ....

e-mail: ....

x. Name and address of the bookseller from whom you have purchased this book:

....

....

....

xi. Name and address of the library where you would like to find the book:

....

....

xii. Name and address of your institution (Please mention the University or Board):

....

....

xiii. Your name, e-mail, and complete postal address:

....

....

....

xiv. A few other titles published by us that you would like to read:

....

....

The best assessment will be rewarded half-yearly. The award will be in the form of our publications, as decided by the Editorial and Marketing Operations Division, amounting to Rs. 1000/- (Rupees one thousand) only.

....

Please mail the filled up coupon at your earliest to :

Editorial & Marketing Operations Division

NEW CENTRAL BOOK AGENCY (P) LTD

8/1 Chintamoni Das Lane, Kolkata 700 009

West Bengal, INDIA

Ph. No.: 033 + 22418411, 22418573, 22419094

Fax: 033 + 22419573, 22413852

e-mail: ncbapvtltd@eth.net, ncba@cal2.vsnl.net.in

Website: www.centralgroup.com